Danny Siegel's
Bar and Bat Mitzvah
Mitzvah Book

Danny Siegel's
Bar and Bat Mitzvah
Mitzvah Book

A Practical Guide for
Changing the World
Through Your Simcha

by DANNY SIEGEL

THE TOWN HOUSE PRESS
Pittsboro, North Carolina

The thank-yous are numerous and gratefully offered:

From the earliest stages of planning this book, to the final touches, various individuals contributed ideas, refinements, relevant texts and programming ideas. I appreciate their help in sharing in the vision of the benefits of this book. Dr. Abraham and Shulamit Gittelson, Gordon and Myra Gondos, Samantha Abeel, Allan and Merle Gould, Glenn Easton, Arleen, Marc, Joshua and Jonathan Sternfeld, Merrill Alpert, Debbie Wilcox, Dr. Ellen Frankel, Ellen Masters, Michael Rotjan, Mark Stadler, Professor Daniel Sperber, Donna and Ilan Glazer, Sol Levy, Louis Berlin, Allan and Merle Gould, Sandra Barsky Daniels and Sue Ringler Pet, Jody Harburger, Rena Draiman, Dr. Eliezer Jaffe, Aaron Lansky, Alyssa Beni, Amy Ripps, Dr. Michael Stulberg, Ron and Meryl Gallatin, Rose Robinson, Michael Wolf, Yosef Ben Shlomo Hakohen, Eli Dicker, Cantor Dana Anesi, Susan Goldhaber, and Lori Steigerwald. Many Rabbis shared their wisdom and insights with me, among them: Rabbis Neal Gold, Jack Riemer, Arthur Green, Jonathan Schnitzer, Matthew Simon, Irvin Wise, David Stern, Debra Robbins, Howard Siegel, and Ronald Isaacs. Rabbi Jeffrey Salkin was among the first who wrote that Bar and Bat Mitzvah should have more substance to it. He was — and is — correct, and his writings on the subject have moved many to incorporate Mitzvahs and spiritual elements into their Simchas.

I would like to particularly thank Sharon Halper and Arnie Draiman, my teachers and friends, who offered many useful suggestions. Both wrote the essential material for specific chapters, Sharon about the gifts, and Arnie about the web as a tool for Mitzvahs.

Judy and Steve Kerbel for their careful next-to-last proofreading for typographical errors.

Louise Cohen, master of the English language, offered many useful suggestions both in style and content.

To Lisa Bauch for her wonderful work designing the book and cover.

Many individuals were kind enough to allow me to use the stories of their Mitzvah projects, and I am grateful for their permission to do so. Among them are Ben Goldhaber, Rachel Steigerwald, Lisa Easton, Andrew Cohen, Benjamin Salman, Stefanie Lopatkin, Meryl Innerfield, Abby Kerbel, and Jennifer Titche.

Above all, my thanks to Naomi Eisenberger, who, beyond the contributions of all others, helped me shape the book, and to make certain that I wrote exactly what I meant to express. Much of her expertise comes from innumerable phone calls to B'nai and B'not Mitzvah and their parents to discuss their Mitzvah projects and to direct them to the exact Tikkun Olam they seek.

To the Jewish Publication Society of America for use of their translations of Biblical texts from *Tanakh* (1985), certainly the most accurate שׁ שׁ פ/Pshat translation in the English language. I adapted and changed many of the translations freely according to the needs of the particular context. All of these adaptations and poetic extensions are my own responsibility.

Cover, design, and layout by Lisa Bauch

First Printing 2004

International Standard Book Number: 0-940653-47-8

To Order:
CMS Distributing
Naomike@aol.com

For Louise Cohen

לאה יעטע בת גוטליב ז״ל וחיה שרה, שתחיה

Friend and Teacher

Eloquent, Insightful

Brilliant Mitzvah Thinker

Tireless Mitzvah Maker

שדכנית-Shadchanit, Matchmaker-for-Tikkun-Olam par excellence

Books by Danny Siegel

Mitzvah and Jewish Values

ANGELS (essays), 1980*
GYM SHOES AND IRISES: Personalized Tzedakah, 1981*
GYM SHOES AND IRISES: Book Two, 1987*
MUNBAZ II AND OTHER MITZVAH HEROES, 1988
FAMILY REUNION: Making Peace
   in the Jewish Community, 1989
MITZVAHS, 1990
AFTER THE RAIN (Children's Story for Adults), 1993*
HEROES AND MIRACLE WORKERS, 1997
1 + 1 = 3 AND 37 OTHER MITZVAH PRINCIPLES
   FOR A MEANINGFUL LIFE, 2000
DANNY SIEGEL'S BAR AND BAT MITZVAH
   MITZVAH BOOK: A Practical Guide for
   Changing the World Through Your Simcha, 2004

For Children

TELL ME A MITZVAH
   (Children's stories, Kar-Ben Copies, Inc., 1993)
THE HUMONGOUS PUSHKA IN THE SKY
   (Children's Story, 1993)
MITZVAH MAGIC: What Kids Can Do
   to Change the World (Kar-Ben/Lerner, 2002)

Humor

THE UNORTHODOX BOOK OF JEWISH RECORDS
AND LISTS (humor, co-authored with Allan Gould), 1982

Poetry

SOULSTONED, 1969*
AND GOD BRAIDED EVE'S HAIR, 1976*
BETWEEN DUST AND DANCE, 1978*
NINE ENTERED PARADISE ALIVE, 1980*
UNLOCKED DOORS:
   The Selected Poems of Danny Siegel 1969-1983, 1983*
THE GARDEN, WHERE WOLVES AND LIONS
   DO NO HARM TO THE SHEEP AND DEER, 1985*
THE LORD IS A WHISPER AT MIDNIGHT:
   Psalms and Prayers, 1985
BEFORE OUR VERY EYES:
   Readings for a Journey Through Israel, 1986
THE MEADOW BEYOND THE MEADOW, 1991*
A HEARING HEART, 1992
HEALING: Readings and Meditations, 1999

Midrash and Halachah

WHERE HEAVEN AND EARTH TOUCH:
An Anthology of Midrash and Halachah,
Book One, 1983*; Large Print Edition, 1985*,
Book Two, 1984*, Book Three, 1985*,
Combined Books One-Three, 1988,
Hardback edition (Jason Aronson), 1989; Soft cover, 1995
Source Book: Selected Hebrew and Aramaic Sources, 1985*

*Out of Print

Table of Contents

"Danny Siegel reminds us that doing Mitzvahs is what "empowerment" is really all about! He has written a family guidebook for turning a personal and family Simcha into a world-altering event."

Sharon Halper
Coordinator of Professional Development, BJENY Westchester Center

"Once again Danny Siegel has worked his unique Mitzvah Magic. He not only instructs young people in righteous deeds and giving, but he also empowers them as they approach adulthood to appreciate their ability to change the world. This book should be on every Bar or Bat Mitzvah reading list!"

Rabbi Mark B Greenspan
Beth Shalom Oceanside Jewish Center, Oceanside, New York

"Bar/Bat Mitzvah can be — *should* be — a milestone in a Jewish young person's development. In this timely and crucial book, Danny Siegel helps us insure that moral development is an essential part of that process. Students and families who read the book and learn from it undoubtedly will take their place as Jewish healers of the broken pieces of our world...and isn't that the essence of what Bar and Bat Mitzvah is all about?"

Rabbi Neal Gold
Anshe Emeth Memorial Temple, New Brunswick

"Bar/Bat Mitzvah is something all the children in our synagogues experience yet there isn't one single book dedicated to guiding them through this significant process and giving the experience a decidedly "Mitzvah" orientation. Who better than the "Mitzvah Man" himself - Danny Siegel - to compose such an important educational tool? This book will elevate the Bar/Bat Mitzvah experience for students, parents and teachers."

Rabbi Ed Farber
Beth Torah Adath Yeshurun, North Miami Beach, Florida

What This Book Is All About

I have written this book to serve a variety of purposes. Above all, I want this to be a practical guide for introducing Mitzvahs into any and every aspect of the events that comprise the Bar/Bat Mitzvah celebration. Sections of the book will deal with everything from the speeches to incredibly colorful כיפות/kippot/yarmulkas made by Mayan women in Guatemala, to the content and format of the invitation, centerpieces and whom to honor and how best to honor them. Mitzvah opportunities are to be found everywhere and at any moment. This book provides very concrete suggestions and techniques that will help families decide how to connect Mitzvahs to the celebration. It is at that time that the Bar/Bat Mitzvah will then truly become a Mitzvah experience.

Some of the sections are addressed to the Bar/Bat Mitzvah; others are intended for the parents. All can be shared and discussed as a family.

I have placed very special emphasis on the Bar/Bat Mitzvah's Mitzvah project and how the Bar/Bat Mitzvah can best distribute any Tzedakah money he or she has to change the world. The simple fact is that *hundreds of thousands of lives have been touched because of Bar and Bat Mitzvah Mitzvah projects and Tzedakah money.* I personally believe that the more accurate figure is *millions of lives,* but I wouldn't want my readers to doubt the credibility of this book because they think that I am exaggerating. Nevertheless, I base my estimate on the hundreds of parents, kids, rabbis, cantors, educational directors, teachers, friends, and family members who have told me for years — and continue to tell me — the amazing stories of what they have seen and heard. They have sent me, and continue to send me, dozens and dozens of invitations, announcements, speeches, and newspaper and magazine articles from Mitzvah projects they have seen or read about.

Whatever the true figure, the number of lives that have been changed for the better because of Bar and Bat Mitzvah Mitzvah projects and Tzedakah money is staggering. So many people have food, clothing, shelter, and heat, are not lonely or living in despair, have hope, have a second chance at Life, have Life itself — because of our glorious *kinderlach* who have come of age by sharing their talents and Mitzvah money.

These numbers are all the more staggering when we consider that the Bar and Bat Mitzvah Mitzvah Project idea only really became widespread in the last 10 or 15 years. And these numbers, these people, these human beings include not only the beneficiaries of the Bar/Bat Mitzvah's Mitzvah projects and Tzedakah money, but also those who heard them speak, read about their Mitzvah work, and were, in turn, inspired to increase their own commitment to תיקון עולם/Tikkun Olam, Fixing the World.

In addition, I believe this book will provide a larger, philosophical framework for the Bat/Bar Mitzvah experience. In rather high-sounding language, I call that section of the book "The Larger Picture: Reflections On The Meaning of Family and The Purpose and Meaning of Life." It offers leading questions, exercises, and ideas for reflection at this particular juncture in the life of the child, the family, the Jewish community, and the community at large. It is my intention that this book will help lay the groundwork for moving the Bat/Bar Mitzvah with greater enthusiasm towards a life of Mitzvahs.

It is hoped that reading this book will allow the Bar/Bat Mitzvah and his or her family to not only know *how* to integrate Mitzvahs more meaningfully into the events, but also *why* it is so important to do so.

Some Notes About Terminology and My Own Word Usage

The true linguistic meaning of the term "בר/בת מצוה - Bar/Bat Mitzvah" is **"Mitzvah Person, Mitzvah Man/Mitzvah Woman."** It does *not* mean "son of a Mitzvah" or "daughter of a Mitzvah," both of which are cumbersome and make little sense in English. In fact, it is perfectly correct to say that *someone* is, is becoming, or has become a Bar or Bat Mitzvah, a Mitzvah Person. Furthermore, technically speaking, one is not "Bar/Bat Mitzvahed" by means of a ceremony. On reaching a certain age, a Jewish person becomes quite simply — with no flourish or fuss — and then is, for the rest of his or her life a Bar/Bat Mitzvah, a Mitzvah Man or Mitzvah Woman.

Jewishly speaking, Bar/Bat Mitzvah means Voluntary-Mitzvah-Time is over, and their Real-Live-Mitzvah-Time has begun. Being a Jewish adult means that the Bar/Bat Mitzvah Person has joined the community of people who realize that Life is all about doing Mitzvahs. She or he is publicly proclaiming a readiness to begin to *do* these Mitzvahs, to begin the magnificent journey to make herself or himself and the world a better place *Jewishly*. The Jerusalem Talmud (Terumot 8:5)[1] describes a certain woman as one "who loved the Mitzvah of Tzedakah very much." Ultimately, we would hope to be able to describe the Bar/Bat Mitzvah Person in the same terms, a Lover-of-Mitzvahs.

Becoming a בר/בת מצוה - Bar/Bat Mitzvah means experiencing to the very highest degree the wonders of שמחה של מצוה/Simcha Shel Mitzvah, The Joy of Doing Mitzvahs. This Life-event means comprehending that it is a זכות/Zechut, **a *privilege* to do Mitzvahs.** It is a realization that we have been entrusted with this wondrous holy work, and are empowered with amazing individual Jewish-and-human power to make an enormous impact on the world, Life, other human beings…and on ourselves. As the Rabbanit Bracha Kapach, one of the great Mitzvah heroes of our time, frequently says, "תזכה/תזכי למצות - Tizkeh/Tizkee Lemitzvot, May you have the privilege to do many more Mitzvahs." Those who have been fortunate enough to meet her know that the appropriate response is, "נזכה למצות /Nizkeh Lemitzvot, May we have the privilege of doing many more Mitzvahs together."

The three Hebrew terms I use most frequently are מצות/Mitzvahs, צדקה/Tzedakah, and תקון עולם/Tikkun Olam, Fixing the World.

Tikkun Olam is the easiest to explain. It simply means *doing* something, anything, to fix anything which is wrong in the world or in someone's life.

Tzedakah literally means "justice, doing the right thing." Tzedakah does *not* mean "charity," which is derived from a Latin root meaning "love." In its broadest sense, Tzedakah means we do Tikkun Olam because something is *wrong* or out of balance, and Tzedakah is the commanding force we employ to set things back on track. In its more restrictive sense, Tzedakah means using a prescribed portion of money for the sake of Tikkun Olam.

I use **"Mitzvahs"** two different ways. In Jewish tradition, Mitzvahs are commandments. While secular society stresses voluntary deeds — which certainly have their place — Judaism sees these acts of Tikkun Olam as divine commands which we are expected to follow. In everyday usage, the word "Mitzvot" often has the connotation of all the commandments, both ritual Mitzvahs and Tikkun Olam-type Mitzvahs. They cover relations בין אדם למקום/between human beings and God, and בין אדם לחברו/ between human beings and other human beings. The former includes the peace and wellbeing that come from a fulfilling observance of Shabbat, the significance and appreciation of freedom that comes from a Passover Seder, and studying and reciting the Torah reading and Haftarah at a Bar/Bat Mitzvah.

In this book, I generally use the term "Mitzvahs" in reference to relations between human beings and other human beings; i.e., "good deeds, acts of Tikkun Olam done because they are the right thing to do." This is why I prefer the Yiddish pronunciation "Mitzvahs" rather than "Mitzvot." In Yiddish, it is easy to say "…because it's a Mitzvah," and it is understood that the speaker means "doing a good deed for someone."

One linguistic problem remains: What to call the Bar/Bat Mitzvah person? "Celebrant"? — Stilted, rings phony in the ear. "Emerging-adult," "emerging-Jewish-adult"? Cumbersome. "Child"? Chronologically, yes, but not really descriptive enough or useful in our context. "Young adult" falls short. After thinking about it for many long hours, I have decided occasionally to use the term "kid," the plural being "kids" or, in Yiddish, *"kinderlach"*…but as an absolute term of endearment and praise, as in "those fabulous/glorious *kinderlach*." When I refer to the Bar/Bat Mitzvah as "kids" or *"kinderlach,"* I mean "those incredibly sweet, awesomely won-

4

derful, fine, overwhelmingly generous and bighearted kids." In this book, they are just that: glorious Mitzvah Men and Women.

Read on — make your Bar/Bat Mitzvah the best Mitzvah celebration it can be.

לחיים - **Lechaim! To Life!**

The Larger Picture:

Reflections on

The Meaning of Family

And The Meaning

And Purpose of Life

24 Questions Parents May Wish to Ask Themselves

אַל־תִּמְנַע־טוֹב מִבְּעָלָיו בִּהְיוֹת לְאֵל יָדֶיךָ [יָדְךָ] לַעֲשׂוֹת:

**Do not hold back from doing good for others
When you have the power to do so.** *(Proverbs 3:27)*

Raising a child is lived in small time units. It is so much a day-by-day affair. It is time-consuming beyond anything you imagined when your daughter or son was born, and has been filled with pleasures and worries, highs and lows. Mostly, though, it is been essentially "normal," even-flowing.

Now, though, Bar/Bat Mitzvah is approaching. It may have caught you off guard, and in your mind it may give you a feeling of all-of-a-sudden. This is hardly like the routine of buying new shoes for Rachel, shlepping Max to a baseball game, or driving Shira to school because she overslept and missed the bus.

Bar/Bat Mitzvah is a different class and magnitude of life experience, for your child...and for you as a parent. Simchas/שמחות, joyous family celebrations, are an ideal opportunity to consider and re-think certain momentous real-Life topics that may last have been thought about at your child's birth.

The following are just a few of the possible questions that may be somewhere in the back of your mind and which you might want to active-ly think about as your child is about to enter a brand-new stage of Jewish life. Your Glorious Child is about to become a Mitzvah Person. What does it all mean?

The questions are listed in no particular order of importance:

1. What do I want my child to be when he or she grows up? This question is not about the usual categories of "occupation," "field of endeavor," or "ways to make a living," but rather, what kind of human being and Jew would I want my daughter or son to be? There often is a degree of overlap between "making a living" and "the kind of person someone is." You are asking the question now in order to get to the very heart of the matter: Is being a Mitzvah Person and a Mensch the highest priority or in some way of secondary importance?

2. Have I ever asked myself, "Is my child gifted in Tikkun Olam-type Mitzvahs?" It is hoped that not only you will look for this potential in your child, but also your child's teachers will look. Indeed, if everyone — parents, grandparents, friends, teachers — would look at children for this kind of talent, the sum-total of Mitzvahs and Tikkun Olam in the world would increase exponentially. You are already watching for promise in music, math, sports and the like. Taking note of Mitzvah-talent is of no less importance.

3. When I think about the future development of my child, what do I mean when I say — "There are no guarantees"? In the larger sense, this cliché (as with all clichés) is only a partial truth. "No guarantees" is obviously an aspect of the nature and flow of life. However, even though there are no guarantees, it is possible to ask yourself how you would change the odds, offering your child a better chance to become a Mitzvah-doing-Mensch.

4. What do I mean when I say to myself, "I want the best for my child?" What does "the best" mean? In what contexts and in relation to what other things, people, and events in life do you want your child to be "the best"? What are the ultimate reasons for being "the best"? In which ways is being "the best" an authentic Jewish value, and in which other ways is it not?

5. What do I mean when I say, "I want my child to be happy"?

6. What do I mean when I say, "I want my child to be successful"?

7. Exactly what aspects of my child's personality and activities my child is engaged in make me particularly proud?

8. What do I mean when I say, "I want my child to have what I never had?" Perhaps writing out a list of these opportunities and items will help you to answer this one more completely. Your own list may include things such as "I want them not to be lonely," and "I want them to have a close, loving relationship with me" if these were missing in your own life. Asking this question and the previous one should help parents focus more on their child as a separate person, and helps the parents avoid the pitfall of "living through their children."

9. When I say to myself or to my child, "Count your blessings" — what exactly do I mean? The Talmud teaches that every Jew should recite 100 blessings every day. (Menachot 43b)[2] It might be worthwhile at this time to make a list of what you consider to be 100 of your personal blessings...and to ask yourself, "Does my child understand what these blessings are in my life and why I consider them to be blessings? Ask your child to make a list for her or his own life's blessings.

10. Have I discussed my own Mitzvah work with my child and other family members?

11. Have I spoken to my child about where I give my Tzedakah money, and how I decide where and how much to give. Have I taught this child that there are really two different *kinds* of money in his or her life: (a) personal money and (b) Tzedakah money?

12. Have I told my child that I am donating to Tzedakah in honor of his or her becoming a Mitzvah Person?

13. What is the relationship between my child's education and what kind of a person he or she is and will possibly become? Does it contribute to his or her Jewish and human character (in Yiddish – מענטשלעכקייט/"Menschlichkeit")?

14. What is the relationship between my child's *Jewish* education and what kind of a person he or she is and will possibly become? Does it contribute to his or her essential character (in Yiddish – "Menschlichkeit ")?

15. Do you expect your child's Bar/Bat Mitzvah and Bar/Bat Mitzvah Mitzvah Project to contribute towards her or his becoming a Mensch? Is there an *automatic, potential,* or a *possible* connection between doing Mitzvahs and becoming/being a Mensch?

16. If my child came home with a 97 or 98 on an exam or paper, did I ever ask him or her, "What did you get wrong?" (And did my parents do the same to me, too?) Is this the best approach to teaching my child The Ultimate Meaning of Education, Menschlichkeit, Torah, Mitzvahs, Tikkun Olam, Being Jewish? What would be a healthier approach to getting good grades?

17. Jewish tradition teaches, "Mitzvahs were given in order to refine human beings" (Leviticus Rabba 13:3)[3]. As my child becomes a Bat/Bar Mitzvah, what qualities would I like to see "refined out" of her/his personality, (i.e., the superficial, the silly, the meaningless, etc.)? What qualities would I like to see remain, appear, or become predominant in my child?

18. Who are my child's heroes? Are Mitzvah heroes a significant part of his or her understanding of what a teacher is? Do they understand that learning from these Giants of Tikkun Olam can play a crucial part in his or her life? Does my child make the connection that, in some way, this is the kind of person he or she may want to be when he or she "grows up"?

19. Who are my child's friends? What kind of חברה/*chevra* — the group he or she spends the most time with — is this group of friends? Are they "into" doing Mitzvahs?

20. (Not a question) Finish the sentence (when addressing my child), "You should use all of your [God-given] gifts for…." Parents and child should *all* finish that sentence and discuss their answers.

21. You are probably saying to yourself, "How did this happen so quickly? It seems like not so long ago my child was just born/crawling/speaking/walking/entering kindergarten?" The non-question is: Finish the sentence, "Life is short, therefore..." Have your child do the same and compare and discuss your answers. Friends and students have also suggested that it may be equally productive to finish the sentence, "Life is long, therefore…" Your answers may include, "Therefore there is time to change who I am and what I do with my time and Self" and "Losing friends because they drift away is terrible, but life is long, there is time to make new, true friends."

22. How seriously do I take my own commitment to Judaism and things Jewish? For example, in the area of Torah study, does my child see me engaged in personal study and Torah classes? Jewish tradition actually teaches (Shulchan Aruch, Yoreh De'ah 245:2)[4] that adult education takes precedence over that of children. There are many reasons for this ruling, but one of the most important ones is that without Torah knowledge, how will a parent teach the child?

An appropriate analogy from air travel comes to mind. The flight attendant says, "In the event of loss of oxygen, put on your oxygen mask first, *then* put one on your child." When we first hear this, it doesn't sound right. On second thought, though, we understand that this makes perfect sense, and is really the "normal" way to react in an emergency. A dysfunctional adult deprived of oxygen if of no use to the child. So, too, "normal" thinking gives precedence to adult education. But as we know, children are very perceptive. They learn very quickly if Mommy or Daddy just drops them off at Hebrew School and picks them up afterwards. It "feels" to them like it's a burden for the parent to *shlep* them back and forth. They also get the message *very* quickly when religious school classes take second place to other outside activities.

23. How seriously do I take my own dedication to Tikkun Olam, and if I am serious about it and actively commit to Mitzvah projects, do I do it alone, or with my family, or both?

24. Does my image of being a role model for my child approximate my child's perception of me? Does my daughter or son see me as deep, thoughtful, superficial, silly, workaholic, generous with my time and money, loving, distant, (sadly) irritable at work and pleasant at home or pleasant and irritable at home?

A classic example of a child "getting" it is the story of a fisherman named Tuck Donnelly. While working as a manager on a commercial fishing vessel, one of Tuck Donnelly's crew members told him how distressed he was about how much fish they had to throw back — dead or alive. Perfectly good protein that could feed hungry

Americans was being wasted. Because of government regulations, they were allowed to keep only pollock and cod. After many meetings and long negotiations, Donnelly succeeded in having the government change the regulations and now his Mitzvah project, SeaShare, has become a supplier of millions of pounds of fish to food banks, soup kitchens, and shelters around the country. Commercial vessels and processors have come "on board," and many thousands of Americans are eating more healthy food due to SeaShare's efforts. It's a wonderful Mitzvah story, to be sure.

The question remains, do Mr. Donnelly's children "get it"? Do they know what Daddy is "all about"? The answer is a most definite Yes, and the proof is that one day, Mr. Donnelly's wife, Jax, overheard a conversation between their daughter, Rachel and two friends. The first one said, "My Dad's a lawyer, and he makes a lot of money." The second one said, "My Dad's a doctor, and he makes a lot of money." Rachel's words say it all — "My Dad feeds hungry people."

A Good Heart — Priceless

הקדוש ברוך הוא ליבא בעי

The Holy One wants your heart. *(Sanhedrin 106b)*

חֲכַם־לֵב יִקַּח מִצְוֹת

The person who has a wise heart does Mitzvahs. *(Proverbs 10:8)*

Jewish tradition has much to say about the importance of being a goodhearted person. For example, the Talmud teaches us (Sanhedrin 106b) "הקדוש ברוך הוא ליבא בעי" - The Holy One wants your heart." Furthermore, centuries ago, the distinguished Torah teacher, Rabban Yochanan Ben Zakkai asked his five favorite students (Pirke Avot, Chapter 2), which I paraphrase, "If you had to choose the single most important human quality to have, which one would it be?" The students, Torah-giants all of them, answered variously: a good friend, a good neighbor, the ability to see the consequences of one's actions, a good eye....These are all certainly good answers, the last one definitely being open to many rich interpretations. But the teacher's favorite answer was that given by Rabbi Elazar Ben Arach, "לב טוב/a good heart," because, as Rabban Yochanan Ben Zakkai explained, all the other qualities are included in having a good heart.

The modern Hebrew language continues in that vein. According to the Even Shoshan Hebrew dictionary, the standard modern Hebrew-Hebrew dictionary, there are approximately 225 common word combinations, compounds, and idioms that use the word "לב/heart." While English does not nearly have as many, we have several positive terms, such as to hearten, heart-of-hearts, heartwarming, wholehearted, lighthearted; as well as negatives: hardhearted, heartache, heartsick, heartrending, and heartbroken...and, of course, "heartbreak" as in Elvis Presley's famous lyric to "take a walk down Lonely Street to Heartbreak Hotel."

If you are on the look-out for examples and you attune yourself to listening for stories of the primacy of this human quality, you will find them everywhere. My friend, Glenn Easton, once sent me an article about Nickole Evans, a high school student in Kennewick, WA, who has established quite a reputation for her many acts of goodness and kindness to others. In this article, she is quoted as follows, ***I'm not the smartest girl in*** *the world, nor am I the most talented. What I have is a heart."*

Another example: A few years ago, I was the guest speaker for graduation at the Solomon Schechter High School on Long Island. One of the speeches was delivered in Hebrew by Hila Ratzabi, a graduating senior, who had prepared the speech with three other students. Parts of the speech included the following: *The unique character of our school has given us the tools to become* בעלי ידע ורחמנות - *knowledgable,* **compassionate** *Jews....***We have learned to care about the community and to take action in the name of Tikkun Olam***....We have grown as a group, but, more importantly, we have grown as informed, open-minded,* **caring** *individuals who will make a difference in the future.* [My emphases.] For "caring," Hila carefully chose to use the Hebrew "טובי לב," literally, "good-hearted." *Now* the parents really knew that all their time, effort, and money that they had invested in their child's education made perfect sense.

I was ecstatic, and had there been a way to hug all 17 graduates, the principal, and the teachers without interrupting the ceremony, I most definitely would have done so. Hearing those beautiful words, any Jewish educator would have felt fulfilled.

A popular TV advertisement for MasterCard credit cards is a wonderful illustration of these kinds of values. With some adaptation and reworking on my part, it goes something like this:

A very professional TV voice says,

"Paying for dancing lessons so you can dance with your wife like a *Mensch* and instead of the clumsy embarrassing dance partner you were in college — $237.00."

"Two tickets for a 10-day cruise to the Caribbean far away from your kvetchy *kinderlach,* through the Panama Canal (and, hopefully, eventually back) — $3,500, not counting all the tips."

"Gazing into your wife's eyes while dancing with ease on the deck in the full moonlight to the sound of your favorite Vietnam Anti-War songs by Bob Dylan — *Priceless."*

This is how it might sound (you supply the pictures yourself) in relation to the Bar/Bat Mitzvah events:

Mom's and Dad's voices alternating:

"Paying for the veggie chopped liver, vegetable dip, herring tidbits, and low-fat, sugar-free cookies for the *nosh* after services in synagogue — $37.25."

"Putting Cuddles, your Great Dane, in the kennel for the week-end so he won't slobber on all the relatives, friends, and other invited guests — $85.00."

"Seeing your child stand before the congregation and declare by word and deed his or her readiness to be a Mitzvah Person until the age of 120 — *Priceless."*

Yet another example: a friend took me into a hippie-ish type of store where, among other interesting items, there were funny bumper stickers, refrigerator magnets, and post cards with brief, clever phrases, the kind that are intended to be pearls of wisdom and beacons of light in Life. Most of the cards were on the order of "Don't count your chickens…" and "Time heals all wounds," but one really caught my eye. It was by Elizabeth David, who, according to various search engines is a famous British food writer. Her wonderfully concise and thought-provoking line:

"There are people who take the heart out of you,
and there are people who put it back."

Very nice. One might say it really gets to the heart of the matter.

In one particular instance in Yiddish, we also find clear evidence of the heart's importance. It appears in conjunction with the way the mind functions. Yeho'ash's famous Yiddish translation of the Torah produced a most astonishing word. In the book of Exodus, the Hebrew word-combination חכם-לב combines "חכם," meaning "wise," and occasionally "smart, bright," with "ל ב/heart." Yiddish, based in part on an older form of the German language, often combines two or more words into one. Yeho'ash's word, קלוגהארציג/Klughartzig brings the two concepts so closely together, they have become one. קלוג/Klug means "smart" and "הארץ/Hartz" means "heart." As I understand the word קלוגהארציג/Klughartzig, it means that whatever our intellectual gifts, we should use them *only* if they are first filtered through the human heart.

Being goodhearted is a critical value for human beings. Our mind's intelligence, talents, imagination, and creativity are best used when they are filtered through our heart's abilities to care. These values can best be summarized by various free interpretations of the Biblical verse in The Book of Proverbs 10:8, חֲכַם־לֵב יִקַּח מִצְוֹת. Without going into the linguistic difficulties of the words, we have three essential elements of "wisdom/intelligence," "heart," and "Mitzvahs."

Allowing for my very free translation of this difficult verse, we can summarize the entire concept contained in these four Hebrew words: A person who uses his or her קלוגהארציקייט/Klughartzigkeit will make Mitzvahs a significant part of his or her life. My friends, students, and teachers have offered additional meaningful interpretations: (1) The truly wise, goodhearted person embraces Mitzvahs; (2) The person who knows how to connect the mind to the heart integrates Mitzvahs into his or her very being; (3) Those who "get it" — that goodheartedness is of fundamental importance will choose to do a multitude of Mitzvahs; (4) People who are doing Mitzvahs for others will, in turn, know how to be a recipient of the goodhearted acts of others — others will want to do them for you because of the kind of person you are, and, finally, (5) Those people who know the supreme importance of doing Mitzvahs may possibly be able to comfortably accept them from others. Giving people have been empathizing with the needs of others and may better recognize when they, themselves, are in need. Simply by connecting the mind and heart the right way, the human possibilities seemed endless.

From a practical standpoint, it might be a useful exercise for you to discuss with your child the comparative importance of intelligence and kindness. Use as many of the "heart" words and phrases as possible in the conversation, such as "soft-hearted," "wearing your heart on your sleeve," and "heartless." Relate it to the forthcoming Bar/Bat Mitzvah and express your hope that the Bar/Bat Mitzvah experience, and especially the Bar/Bat Mitzvah Mitzvah Project experience, will reinforce the supreme importance of this human quality. It is hoped that the message will come through not only for the Bar/Bat Mitzvah, but for parents and all others who participate in the experience as well.

A fine conclusion to this exercise would be for you and your child to make a list of all the good-hearted people you know. This will add that final touch of clear perspective to what it is to become a Mitzvah Man or Mitzvah Woman.

On the Need For Your Child (And Everyone Else) To Meet, Hang Out With, Work With, And Learn From, Mitzvah Heroes

Charismatic leaders make us think,
"Oh, if only I could do that, be like that."
True leaders make us think,
"If they can do that, then...I can too." *(John Holt, Educator)*

וְצַדִּיק יְסוֹד עוֹלָם
The very foundation of the world is Good People. *(Proverbs 10:25)*

כשהצדיק בעיר הוא זיוה והוא הודה והוא הדרה
When The Good Person is in a community,
that person is its radiance, its glory, and its brilliance.
(Ruth Rabbah 2:12)

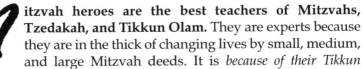

itzvah heroes are the best teachers of Mitzvahs, Tzedakah, and Tikkun Olam. They are experts because they are in the thick of changing lives by small, medium, and large Mitzvah deeds. It is *because of their Tikkun Olam work* that they have a profound understanding of caring, power, the nature of people as human beings. For some people (myself included), they may even have the answer to the question, "What is the meaning of life?"....Life is Mitzvahs. They might state it in different words, such as, "Some want to first understand all of the Why of It All and then to act. It is really the other way around. You *do. You* hold the hand of the lonely person; *you* spoon-feed an Elder who can no longer feed herself or himself, you pay a scholarship at a swimming pool or therapeutic horseback riding for someone damaged by a stroke so he or she can have a better chance at 100% rehabilitation. You *do* those things, and *after* you have done them, *then* you will know the Why of It All? If you ask and ask and spend years asking, you may have missed out."

If it is the nature of Mitzvah heroes to be Tikkun Olam teachers, we ought to meet them, hang out with them, work with them, and, as a consequence of the *doing*, learn from them. To analogize: For those looking for the right graduate school, the student looks for two things — the right kind of program *and* certain specific professors who are the best in their field. A master's in drama might lead you to two choices — a program that stresses academics, or one that teaches everything about hands-on acting, playwriting, and stage sets. Having chosen which category of drama program, you have to pick the program where the absolutely right professor for your own specific needs teaches. Certainly, then, if the field of endeavor is Fixing the World, What Makes Good People Good, Life Itself, and the Meaning of Life, the wise decision would be to meet Mitzvah heroes, and do Tikkun Olam the way they do it.

Throughout this book, I write about several of my own Mitzvah heroes. You will become familiar with names like Anita Shkedi, Barbara Bloom Silverman, and Avshalom Beni. Their work is described on my Ziv Tzedakah Fund website, www.ziv.org. You and your daughter or son may already know some Mitzvah heroes, or will discover others through your research. All of them are extraordinary teachers of Tikkun Olam.

During the Bar/Bat Mitzvah period, it is particularly important for the B'nai/B'not Mitzvah to surround themselves with and attach themselves to Mitzvah heroes. There are several reasons for this, among them being:

1. This is probably the first time your child is launching a major Mitzvah project and donating substantial Tzedakah money. He or she may find himself or herself suddenly "rich." Very real guidance and expertise is needed.

2. Even if it is not the first time, this is the first time your child is doing a Tikkun Olam project as the center of attention, and the first time as a Mitzvah Person *required* to do Mitzvahs — a brand-new Mitzvah Person.

3. This is a time when parents may be re-considering the meaning of "wanting the best for their children." I believe that education without Mitzvah-education is incomplete. Since the best teachers of Mitzvahs in the world are not the theoreticians, but rather the Mitzvah heroes, Bar/Bat Mitzvah time is a perfect occasion for meeting them.

4. It may be — for whatever reason — that until now, parents haven't noticed that their child has a very real talent for Mitzvahs. Meeting and working with Mitzvah heroes will bring this more clearly to the parents' attention and give parents a new perspective of the heart, soul, and spirit of a son or daughter. The Mitzvah hero's "job" as teacher is to discover, draw out, develop, and nurture this Mitzvah talent…and to share it with the parents.

5. For whatever reason, it may be that, until now, parents haven't made an effort to look at this child to see if she or he has a very real talent for Mitzvahs. Meeting and working with Mitzvah heroes will bring this more clearly to the parents' attention and give parents a new perspective of the heart, soul, and spirit of the son or daughter. The Mitzvah hero's "job" as teacher is to discover, draw out, develop, and nurture this Mitzvah talent… and to share it with the parents.

6. Jewish tradition (Proverbs 22:6) teaches,

חֲנֹךְ לַנַּעַר עַל־פִּי דַרְכּוֹ גַּם כִּי־יַזְקִין לֹא־יָסוּר מִמֶּנָּה׃

which I translate:

Teach your child Mitzvahs at least as much
as Torah and the "realities of life"
in a way so individualized to his or her needs
that long into the future
the values he or she is taught
will remain a part of his or her very essence and being.

Mitzvah heroes are not only "experts in their field," but they also have another priceless value — they *always* relate to their students as individuals with unique needs, personalities, and talents.

7. This is one of those times when parents review their child's past and look to the future. They may be weighing again the meaning of the phrase, "There are no guarantees...." Having your child meet, hang out, work with, and learn from Mitzvah heroes helps to change the odds in favor of The Good Life, i.e., The Giving, and Therefore, Meaningful Life, for your child.

8. Even if you and your child do not communicate well, the message of Mitzvahs, Tzedakah, and Tikkun Olam may come through clearly, and without the too-often-whined child/parent baggage, "Mom, Dad, you are always telling me what to do." Just maybe there will be some relief, and new lines of communication will be opened.

What Your Child Will Learn From Being With And Working With Mitzvah Heroes

There are so many things your child will learn from meeting Mitzvah heroes, hanging out with Mitzvah heroes, working with Mitzvah heroes and, as a consequence, learning from Mitzvah heroes, I have to list them 1-2-3 as I did above. They will learn —

1. That there is a difference between a job/making a living, and a Jewish person's real occupation: Mitzvahs. Winston Churchill said it most eloquently, "We make a living by what we get, but we make a life by what we give." Your child does not have to grow up to be a Mitzvah hero. That would not be the worst thing that could happen to your daughter or son, but it is a very high goal to achieve. Nevertheless, he or she will know that whatever he or she *does* to make a living, this Bar/Bat Mitzvah-Mitzvah Person *can* be using his or her talents for Mitzvahs both in and outside a job.

This may be a good time to teach your child about various individuals in the community who successfully demonstrate the ability to combine "work" work with Mitzvah work. Since many of these people prefer to do their Mitzvah work quietly, you don't have to name names. But you can tell them about attorneys who take on *pro bono* cases, physicians who are on call to treat uninsured patients, TV producers who create powerful documentaries about Mitzvah heroes and Tzedakah projects, business people who donate goods for new immigrants just getting established in their new homes, and similar Mitzvah-oriented people. It would be good for your child to know of these people early on in life. It may help your son or daughter come to a realization that Mitzvah work is the *real* work in Life.

2. That he or she is *always* capable of great acts of Tikkun Olam, greater than he or she ever thought possible. Whatever her or his own talents, likes and dislikes, stamina, wisdom, and insight, the possibilities are very great. Very similar to the Mitzvah hero's vision and insatiable desire to do Mitzvahs, *everybody* has something inside of himself or herself to make acts of Tikkun Olam very real. John Holt, the educator, said it best, "Charismatic leaders make us think, 'Oh, if only I could do that, be like that.'" True leaders make us think, "'If they can do that, then...I can too.'"

3. That real power is Mitzvah-power and your child may, indeed, become Mitzvah-power hungry the more she or he grows into her or his true self as בר/בת מצוה - Bar/Bat Mitzvah, a Mitzvah Person.

4. That there are different kinds of happiness, fun, joy, satisfaction in Life. The Hebrew term שמחה של מצוה/Simcha Shel Mitzvah, The Joy of Doing Mitzvahs is a unique feeling that penetrates deep into the soul and is among the most profound human emotions and worthwhile experiences in Life. שמחה/Simcha means "affirming life," and its "mere" four Hebrew letters contain within them enthusiasm and an intense passion to live Life fully as a Mitzvah Person. My teacher, and the inspiration of millions of people, the late Rabbi Abraham Joshua Heschel, ז"ל, stated it most eloquently when he wrote, "Living is not a private affair of the individual. Living is what man does with God's time, what man does with God's world."

5. That it is possible to be an awesome, yet humble, human being. They may learn, in fact, that humility is a crucial part of the Mitzvah hero's life. Arrogance and abuse of others is not an acceptable character trait in the world of Mitzvahs, nor is it acceptable in everyday life.

6. That it is possible to live a Life of Mitzvahs and still do "normal" things: go to ball games, the movies and the beach, read books for fun, veg out, channel surf on a flat screen plasma TV, go out to dinner with friends, have as many kinds of fun as there are stars in the sky and grains of sand on the seashore.

7. That Mitzvah heroes are ordinary people. They are not born with any special genius. They are more likely than not just "plain folks." This will teach your child to look at other people in a different way, namely, that each person has an enormous potential for Mitzvahs no matter what a person's official training or degrees, lineage, class status, or

upbringing might be.

8. That since the Mitzvah heroes came to their calling by different means and routes, your child will have a different understanding of Shakespeare's famous line, "...some are born great, some achieve greatness, and some have greatness thrust upon them." (12th Night, Act II, Scene 5) As a result of being with, working with, and learning from the Mitzvah heroes, "greatness" will take on a richer meaning for them.

9. That using one's Tzedakah money and time, effort, and talent for Mitzvahs has infinite possibilities. Meeting the Mitzvah heroes will broaden his or her Tikkun Olam horizons. This is of particular importance at this Bar/Bat Mitzvah moment, since your daughter or son will have more power and Tzedakah money at her or his disposal than ever before.

10. That it is always possible to learn how to use Mitzvah-talents and Tzedakah money more wisely and efficiently.

11. They will learn what *things* are all about. Things can be either טשאַטשקעס/*tchatchkas* or tools. A *tchatchka* is a toy, a plaything, a knick-knack. (Almost) any thing can be either a tchatchka (a toy, a trinket) or it can be a tool, vehicle, or instrument for Mitzvahs. Stated differently: THING → *Thing*-for-good, THING → *Thing*-that-can-make-good-things-happen. For example, a private jet is not in-and-of-itself in any way of negative value. Indeed, many are used in the off hours to transport people cross-country for medical treatments. A Rolls Royce can bring people to synagogue. The most expensive shampoo can give a woman in a shelter that certain glow of dignity that will help her begin the road back to a normal life. A baseball glove given to a lonely kid who has nothing else to hold on to can give him or her hope and the will to live. The poet Marge Piercy expresses why we need a vast array of Mitzvah tools, "What we want to change we curse and then pick up a tool. Bless whatever you can with eyes and hands and tongue. If you can't bless it, get ready to make it new." We just need to keep our eyes open, look at *things,* and *think tool/vehicle/instrument-for-Mitzvahs.*

In Conclusion: A Story a Friend E-mailed to Me

You may have heard the old line that no one ever had an epitaph that read, "I'm sorry I didn't get in another day at the office." The following story is essentially the exact opposite: A recent project in the Springfield, Massachusetts, Jewish community was to photograph and catalogue the gravestones in various cemeteries in the community. By the time that particular article had been written, more than 3,000 gravestones had been documented. One inscription in Yiddish describes a woman by the name of Chiyena Rachel Chaitowsky as "A woman who fed hungry people all the days of her life." That says it all.

Getting A's And/Or Being a Mensch: 2 Polls

ולהוי אנא פקידא בגו צדיקיא
"Allow me, [O Holy One], to be counted among The Good People."
(Zohar 2:206, Siddur)

uring my formal lectures, as well as in private conversations, I have often asked parents, "What would you like your children to be when they grow up?" In various orders, the four most common answers are: "happy," "healthy," "a Mensch," and "Jewish."

In my talks as well as in private conversations, I have asked thousands of teen-agers, "What single thing could you do at this stage of life to please your parents the most?" The near-universal answer: "Get good grades." And they usually answer very quickly and spontaneously.

When I review these two polls in front of an audience, you can feel a certain uneasiness in the air. I usually break the tension with a joke from the not-well-enough-known and too-often-remaindered classic of Jewish humor, *The Unorthodox Book of Jewish Records & Lists* (authors, Allan Gould and yours truly), "The Smartest Jewish Grandchild: Harold Weinstock of River Junction, Missouri, grandson of Earl and Anne Grossinger of Teaneck, New Jersey, recited the Four Questions of the Passover Service *at birth.*" There are three jokes in the chapter, concluding with Sharon Firestone who *"at the age of five weeks* began her own petition to fire the rabbi." We get some good laughs out of this lampooning of precociousness. Then return to the issue at hand.

There is a very serious disparity in the results of these two informal polls. What could possibly explain it? Numerous people have offered possible reasons. One reason they give is, that since the polls were not taken by the standard rules of poll-taking and statistical analysis, it could very well be a false result. Other possibilities suggested include: The people polled may not have constituted a truly random sample; the question may not have been accurately phrased and may have led to "the answers that Danny Siegel wanted to hear," and finally, the same teen-agers I asked may not be the same children of the parents I asked. Their own children may, indeed, know that their parents want them to be happy, healthy, a Mensch, and Jewish. I suspect that the last reason is extremely unlikely. I have asked thousands of teen-agers. The sheer size of my sample leaders me to believe the answers given reflect a fundamental problem we need to face squarely.

In truth, I wish the results were different. But since they aren't, we have to make some sense of them, and *do* something about this enormous disparity. However the message has become central in their thinking, the teen-agers are swept up in the pursuit of excellence and achievement, and the sensation of competitiveness for good grades is often brutal. Inevitably, it takes a toll on the teen-agers' wellbeing.

I remember reading an interesting phrase in a newspaper long ago — "the prison of excellence." When excellence has no context, I think this reporter's phrase is extremely appropriate. To illustrate: Certainly in the world of sports, The Olympic Games are a prominent example of competitiveness. The motto of The Games is *"citius, altius, fortius,"* Latin for "faster, higher, stronger," and the rewards are gold, silver, and bronze medals. The question remains — "context": For the victors, what is the greater, the *ultimate* significance of "getting the gold"? The day after the Olympics, few people even remember who won the silver medal. As for the bronze — we usually only read about them in the record books. And for those athletes who did not even place first, second, or third, what is the *ultimate* meaning of losing?

At this point, I need to make myself absolutely clear, since many people in the past have misinterpreted my words. Some have even taken offense. I am *not* saying, either explicitly or implicitly, that being a straight-A student and being a Mensch are a contradiction in terms. That is why this chapter is called "Getting A's *And*/Or Being a Mensch." Nor am I saying that there is something *essentially* wrong in getting good grades. I am only trying to interpret the results of these two polls. I want to understand the underlying forces that reflect themselves in the emphasis, values, and priorities relating to grades and *Menschlichkeit.*

A מעשׂה/*Myseh,* a real-live story: In the summer of 2000, I was studying with my Ziv Tzedakah Fund summer interns in Israel when, out of the blue, I asked the question, "Which of our Mitzvah heroes do you think has the highest IQ?" The minute I asked, all of us were taken aback. It was such an irrelevant question, and even though we spent no more than 5 minutes going down the list, we remained uncomfortable about it. It really had nothing to do with their Mitzvah work, *absolutely nothing.* What difference, at all, would it make in their awesome Tikkun Olam activities and projects? Even now, reflecting back 3 1/2 years, I wonder why I asked it at all. And even stranger is this: I began my work with Mitzvah heroes in 1975. A full quarter of a century had passed before the thought even occurred to me to ask, and having asked it then, I don't think it will ever come up again in any future conversation.

Now, we need to deal with this issue of Getting A's *And*/Or Being a Mensch.

Indeed, I believe we need to deal with this issue, and, I believe we need to deal with this issue *Jewishly*.

Jewishly, the first point to consider is that that there are no Talmudic terms for "excellence," "achievement," and "competitiveness." While the Rabbis of the Talmudic era *did* have the term "יצר הרע/Yetzer HaRa," it meant the human inclination to do the wrong thing. Competitiveness was only one aspect of the Yetzer HaRa, and the term itself is negative. Competitiveness as a single concept would not have been part of their thinking.

I believe the rabbis' understanding of these concepts would be that, without a connection to some kind of *values,* the terms had no ultimate meaning. For them, to say that someone should achieve excellence because a person should achieve excellence would make no sense. Concerning all three of these terms, I believe they would have asked, "Be excellent, be competitive, achieve — for what purpose? To what end?"

Even nowadays, if you were to ask in slightly literary Hebrew, "For what purpose?" you would say, "לשם מה?/Leshaym Mah?" Someone attuned to the language would then expect to hear "לשם שמיים/Leshaym Shamayim, For the sake of Heaven," meaning "for some higher purpose."

If, for example, we are competitive when we have to raise large sums of emergency Tzedakah funds for a recent catastrophe somewhere in the world, *that* is לשם שמיים/For the sake of Heaven. The same is true for a sense of achievement — we are entitled to feel good for having made this effort and achieving our goal.

For another example, "achievement" might mean that a community achieved the goal of making certain that *everyone in the community* had enough money to make a decent Passover Seder.

The ultimate example for "excellence" is the Mitzvah work of David Copperfield. Copperfield (a.k.a. David Kotkin, Bar Mitzvah at Neve Shalom in Metuchen, NJ) is certainly the most famous magician and illusionist in the world. His Mitzvah project is called Project Magic, and it is used in more than 1,000 hospitals around the world. Occupational and physical therapists employ his special method of teaching simple magic to people in various stages of rehabilitation in order to strengthen their dexterity and improve their motor use. Being the center of attention and performing for others also clearly adds to their motivation and self-image. The end result of Project Magic is that thousands of people can now feed themselves. More important, thousands clean themselves, and avoid the humiliation of having others help them with their bodily needs.

The favorite part of the story is this: Copperfield says, ***"There is nothing I do that is more important."*** A perfect statement from The Best in the World.

In the context of Bar/Bat Mitzvah, excellence should not, therefore, be determined by the fact that he or she recited the blessings fluently, though that is important to a certain extent and very nice. As mentioned in another section of this book, I have never really been comfortable with well-wishers telling the Bar/Bat Mitzvah, "Good job!" It just feels to me like the wrong phrase. The appropriate Jewish phrase would be, "יישר כח - Yishar Koach, All the more strength to you [to live a wonderful life of Mitzvahs]." According to the latest Talmudic dictionaries, the root of the word "יישר" is "ש-ר-ר" – the very same root that gives us the word "שריר - muscle." With your encouragement, the Bar and Bat Mitzvah *kinderlach* are building their constitution to its optimum strength and efficiency to prepare them for a life filled with idealistic good deeds.

The praise of excellence really ought to be: That the Bar/Bat Mitzvah has brilliantly achieved the goal of fully joining the Jewish community as a full-fledged 100% Mitzvah Person.

Returning to the poll of the parents and their answer that they want their child to be a Mensch, let me conclude with some excellent Jewish terms that help us define and articulate what we really want the teen-agers to grow up to be: מענטשלעך/**Menschlich,** best translated as "a decent, caring human being (and much more); ערלעך/**Ehrlich,** honest; פיין/**Fein,** just like it sounds, a fine human being; שיין/**Shayn,** meaning beautiful, as in "a beautiful human being"; זים/**Ziess,** sweet; איידל/**Aydel,** noble, as in "a person who has a noble soul"; to have תמימות/**Temimut** — a powerful word meaning simplicity, innocence, and humility; to embody the principle of "תוכו כברו/**Tocho KeVaro**" — one's inner being is the same as one's outward behavior, and from Turkish Ladino — the self-explanatory terms for a Mensch…"hombre bueno/mujer buena" or "precioso/preciosa."

Perhaps with the approach of this important Jewish milestone of Bar/Bat Mitzvah, there is an excellent opportunity to discuss what you, as parents, *really,* do expect of your child.

To state it in Yiddishized English syntax — Your child should only grow up to be happy, healthy, a Mensch, and a Jew….all four of them, not three, not two, not just one of them.

2 Things _Not_ To Say To Your Child

To be Jewish is to be an idealist. *(Unknown Source)*

*D*uring my lectures, I might mention that I would hope that parents do not say to their children, "Life is not black and white. Life is about gray." I respond quietly, but what I really mean to say is, "*Some* aspects of Life are *not* black and white! Doing Mitzvahs, caring for other people, Tzedakah, doing the right thing *is* all white!" My emphasis really demands three or four exclamation marks. I might continue by saying, "It would be better to communicate to younger people that the non-gray areas are ones we should study and embrace as we live day by day, through hours when we are bombarded with gray moments and experiences." To use a common image: Dusk is a dangerous time to drive. As the world slides into darkness, the wise driver puts on headlights and dispels the oncoming darkness. So, too, with Tzedakah and Tikkun Olam.

During my lectures, I might also mention that I would hope that parents do not say to their children, "It's all right to be idealistic for now. You're young. But when you get older, you'll see there's a Big Real World out there. You'll just have to adjust and be more practical." I meet in my audiences parents and grandparents who are old enough to have participated in the Civil Rights Movement. They may have demonstrated against the War in Vietnam, and possibly did a two-year stint in the Peace Corps in some remote part of the world, where they touched and rebuilt many lives. They, in particular, know about the People Power that can change the course of history and reverse the downspin of personal and community despair. They, in particular, should know better than others not to talk about idealism that way.

And people who are Jewishly informed should also know that Judaism is all about idealism *throughout* life, that things *can* and *will* change for the better. To be Jewish is to be an idealist. To be Jewish is to *act* on that idealism. That is the meaning of Tikkun Olam – we *can* all fix the world, every one of us. Life doesn't have to stay — nor does it really stay — the same forever. *Encourage* your child's idealism.

I can think of no better example than Jennifer Titche's Mitzvah project, Dream Reading. A student in the religious school of Temple Emanuel in

Grand Rapids, Michigan, she once visited a local elementary school, and it seemed to her that she had more books in her own library than the school had in its library. This surprised and shocked her, and, as often happens with such moments, it also opened her eyes. Here was a possibility for her to *do* something. She launched Dream Reading to ask for donations of books and money for libraries for schools that, to her, just didn't have enough of what every kid should have to read.

The first report, December, 2002, that Jennifer mailed to donors and friends stated that she had received 200 donations, over $6,700, and more than 400 books. To quote from her report, "My short term goal as of right now is to get $10,000." Her second report a year later listed more than 340 donations totaling $11,026.65, with 1,263 new books and 1,426 used books donated. In that one year alone she had increased the number of donated books by 2,299. Jennifer's *new* short-term goal was to raise *$20,000.*

This is very impressive indeed. More impressive to adults (who may not be as computer savvy as younger people), Jennifer launched a website, www.dreamreading.org, to extend her reach. Even more impressive is that she launched the project starting when she was 9 years old, a "mere" 4th-grader. *Most* impressive is my favorite line from her first report. "My long term goal is to help all the schools in the world that need help to get books in their libraries." Jennifer's words are not only moving and inspirational, but worth considering as a more correct understanding of the Way of the World, because her idealism has led her to a plan of action. So be it.

I would think the "realists" might want to keep their distance. If we stand by Jennifer, join her in her Tikkun Olam work, and continue to encourage her, she should remain as idealistic as she is now for all her days. *That's* the Jewish approach… at least in my opinion.

In fact, I have been asked on many occasions if I believe that the world is ultimately fixable. My answer is "Yes!" Absolutely. The question also requires a theological response. Will this Ultimate Repair happen by some miraculous act of God, in a flash, an earth-shaking moment? Or will it be by some joint action, a partnership between human beings and God? Being neither a prophet nor a mystic, I have no definitive answer, though I do sense that it will be by partnership. To think otherwise would imply that expending one's best efforts doing Tikkun Olam would be little more than a way to bide one's time until God steps in and makes everything all right. Yes, it *would* be a meaningful way to spend one's days and years, but still it would just be filling time until the heavens opened up. I believe it *because I can feel it in my bones,* and I gain strength from the words of Jennifer Titche and those like her.

To conclude with a story: One of the opposites of "idealism" is "cynicism," a sense that life is essentially not good, not worth repairing. I was once at a meeting at someone's house. One of the hosts made an unmistakably cynical remark. His wife ran to the Tzedakah box and made him put in some money. It was a perfect moment. Something very much out of tune, something not-Jewish had been said. The way to fix the situation was through an act of Tzedakah.

The Family, The Greater Family All the Way Back to Abraham and Sarah, Adam and Eve

כִּי יְדַעְתִּיו לְמַעַן אֲשֶׁר יְצַוֶּה אֶת־בָּנָיו וְאֶת־בֵּיתוֹ אַחֲרָיו
וְשָׁמְרוּ דֶּרֶךְ יְהוָה לַעֲשׂוֹת צְדָקָה וּמִשְׁפָּט

For I have selected him [Abraham]
so that he may instruct his children and his posterity after him
to keep God's ways:
to do what is just and right. [Tzedakah U'Mishpat] *(Genesis 18:19)*

ar/Bat Mitzvah is not only a family celebration. It is an expression of commitment to Jewish living and Jewish values.

The Bar/Bat Mitzvah should be given a strong sense of his or her place in Jewish history, and how this event is part of millennia of Jewish continuity.

An important way to begin the process it to speak with your child about **her or his Jewish name.** Tell your child *why* — out of thousands of choices, you decided to give him or her that specific name, and whether or not the name is in memory or in honor of someone. If your child is named for someone, tell this soon-to-be-full-fledged-Mitzvah-person (or remind him or her) for whom. It is of even greater importance for your son or daughter to know *what kind of person that individual was:* kind, gentle, supportive of others in hard times and times of crisis. For anyone at any age, it should feel like a responsibility and a joy to carry someone else's name as a significant part of what it is to be a person and to be alive.

You may have simply chosen צִיּוֹן/Tzion, Zion/Israel, because of your attachment to Jewish history and Life in Israel, or שׁוֹשַׁנָּה/Shoshana, a rose, because a rose is beautiful and the word itself has a lovely sound. If the name has a meaning in Hebrew (like שׁוֹשַׁנָּה/Shoshana), Yiddish, or Ladino, translate it for them and make it a part of their conscious lives. Mine, for example, is יַעֲקֹב/Ya'akov, Jacob. There is little mystery about that choice. My father, ז"ל, was יצחק/Yitzchak, Isaac, and my older brother, ייבדל לחיים, is אברהם/Avraham. My grandmother, ז"ל, צירעל דבורה/

26

Tzirel Devora, wanted an Abraham, Isaac, and Jacob in the family. Fortunately for me, in addition to this august lineage of ancestors, the name has an uplifting meaning. It is an abbreviated form of אל-יעקב/Ya'akov-El, which means "May God protect," or "God protects."

This is also a good time to double-check for a few special cases for children named for ancestors whose names may have been חיים/Chaim or חיה/Chaya. Both Hebrew words mean "Life." Your grandfather's or great-uncle's name may have been אלטער/Alter ("old" in Yiddish). In all of these cases, these may not have been the original names, but rather were given to the child if he or she were seriously ill. In the Old Country, they often changed the child's name or added these names in order to fool the Angel of Death who would come around looking for a child named Such-and-Such. Because the name was changed, the Angel would not find a "Yosef" or "Rivka" in the house, and would leave the child alone.

Most important, in my opinion, is to emphasize that on this Bar/Bat Mitzvah day, your child will not simply be called up for an עליה/Aliya by a first name. That is for home use, for school, out on the playing fields, and just hanging out with friends. But when it comes time to read the holy message from our Torah, we are *always* connected through our parents, grand-parents, on back through history. In one part my life, I am Danny Siegel, in the other

יעקב יהודה בן יצחק זעליג הלוי ז"ל ויהודית ז"ל
Ya'akov Yehuda ben/son of Yitzchak Zelig HaLevi,
May his memory be for a blessing
and Yehudit,
May her memory be for a blessing.

To further reinforce this sense of Jewish continuity, this might be a good time to work on **the family tree.** Computer programs now make the research and chart-making much easier. Once the diagram is complete, or even partially finished, stress how your child, That Glorious Kid, fits into the charts. They should become aware of the fact that they didn't just spring out of nowhere. (This is analogous to people who think that carrots grow in grocery stores.) You may find that while you are doing this project, you may want to conduct personal interviews with family Elders. Videotape the interviews, à la Spielberg's project for שואה/Shoah, Holocaust survivors. Families need these permanent records, now, and for future generations. In addition, some families have found it meaningful to take their child to the cemetery to visit the graves of his or her ancestors. They will often make rubbings of the epitaphs to keep in a family album at home.

The **geography of family history** is also of particular importance. If your family comes from an Ashkenazi background, it is important to stress your child's European roots. Tell your daughter or son *exactly* why your family is in America (or Canada, England, Australia, etc.). In most family histories, it is because the family, or whatever portion managed to escape, was running away from someone who wanted to kill them. More and more

— and more — the younger generation has little or no "feel" for its European roots. The same applies, of course, to Sefardim and their long journey from Spain and Portugal at the end of the 15ᵗʰ century, through Turkey or Rhodes or Morocco to where you are now living. Yemenite Jews, some Greek Jews, and others have their own unique histories and wanderings. Whatever your family's history, the connection should be made now, as your child becomes Bat/Bar Mitzvah.

The next step takes a little more work. Use your imagination and extend the family tree back to Abraham, beginning with Genesis Chapter 12,"לֶךְ לְךָ - Go forth!", and stress in specific Genesis 18:19, "For I have selected him [Abraham] so that he may instruct his children and his posterity after him to keep God's ways — to do what is just and right. [צדקה ומשפט/Tzedakah U'Mishpat]." And then, only one more step — Go back even farther to Genesis Chapter 1, all the way to the creation of the world and of human beings. Explain in your own words to your child how she or he fits into The Very Large Picture.

Photographs

Three types of photographs may be meaningful in relation to the Bar/Bat Mitzvah events: The Old Ones, The New and Really Good, and The New and Potentially Not-So-Great. The best, in my opinion, is sharing family photo albums beginning with **the Old Ones** — from grandparents' and great-grandparents' generation, as far back as your pictures go. I have found it a valuable exercise every so often to leaf through my grandparents' 50ᵗʰ wedding anniversary album in the late 1940's with its multitude of aunts, uncles, and cousins. It is particularly important to identify and label all relevant dates and names. Remember to include the Hebrew/Yiddish/Ladino names if you can, and the interrelationships to yourselves and your child.

The New and Really Good is at the non-Shabbas party, when many families provide a small, simple camera at each table. I like this very much. Anyone and everyone can fix in time a record of family and friends together at a Simcha, a *community* gathered to share some of Life's joyous moments.

The New and Potentially Not-So-Great is the poster-board-sized display of the Bar Mitzvah Mitzvah Man/Bat Mitzvah Mitzvah Woman. I have noticed this only in recent years, and it definitely has an "up" side: It is a pictorial review of birth to Bar/Bat Mitzvah in many settings and poses. If prepared and arranged with the right touch, this is a lovely new custom. What leaves me a bit unsettled are the displays that are too self-centered on the Bat/Bar Mitzvah, much like party themes entitled, "You are the star!" In my opinion, this misplaced focus can be countered by integrating family pictures (as far back as possible), and photos of the Bar/Bat Mitzvah in community settings. The invention of scanners makes this a very easy touch-up and rescue operation, and would give a much more meaningful context to the exhibit without diminishing the importance of the Bar/Bat Mitzvah. It simply minimizes the risks of too much "Me, Me, Me"-centered view of what a person is supposed to be.

How Your Child and You Fit In

A few paragraphs above, I wrote, "*Explain* in your own words to your child how she or he fits into The Very Large Picture." Now it is time for you to ask your son or daughter to articulate how *he* or *she* sees himself or herself in this long, long line of Jews and human beings. Ask your child to articulate how he or she sees himself or herself *continuing* this Incredible Chain of Being and Jewish Being. At this point, it might be appropriate to have your child answer the question, "What do you want to be when you grow up?" If he or she is willing to make a written statement, that would be even better.

Now for the hard part for some parents — have yourselves answer the question, "What do *I* want to be when I grow up?"…i.e., what you might have written around your own Bat/Bar Mitzvah time of life, and what you mean by "when I grow up" now. For some, this may prove to be a motivating point of departure to consider having an adult Bar or Bat Mitzvah. This might be a very good time to think about it. Some might say (particularly those who have had such an enriching Jewish experience), "Do it!" — whether or not you had one when you were 12 or 13.

Ideally, this could be a family project: Parents and child could compose their answers, even in separate rooms, and share them with each other when they are finished.

One Last Step: Writing an Ethical Will

An ethical will is a written statement about what is and has been important in a person's life…and what values the person wants to pass on to the next generation. This document is an exceptionally fine technique to help your child understand what you and your life are *really* all about. (Unfortunately, children usually find out too much of the story at a שבעה/Shiva for a parent.) Rabbi Jack Riemer's and Nathaniel Stampfer's *Ethical Wills, A Modern Jewish Treasury* is an excellent resource for this project. Since you know your own child best, you should decide at what age to show the ethical will to your daughter or son. Whatever the age, tell your daughter or son now that you are writing this document. In the great chain of your family's Jewish continuity, this will serve as an invaluable document for all who will read it at whatever stage they are in in their own lives.

The Mitzvah-Years Of Our Mitzvah-Lives

Here is the test to find whether your mission on earth is finished. If you're alive, it isn't. *(Richard Bach)*

The 3 Stages of Life According to Jewish Tradition

Many cultures have their own visions of the human life span, and the actual terms they use to describe various stages of life is a key to a people's way of thinking. In English-speaking countries, for example, descriptives such as infant, toddler, child, teen-ager, young adult, adult, mid-life (with or without crisis), empty nester, and retiree indicate many Americans' understanding of the flow of years. In Talmudic times, 1,500 to 2,500 years ago, there were no terms for "teen-ager," "empty nester," or "retiree." This means that they thought about age, growing up, growing older, aging, and the succession of the stages of life differently than we do nowadays. Jewish tradition has several ways to describe the passage of human time. One of my favorites I call "The 3 Stages of Life":

In the very first stage (Niddah 30b)[5], **at the moment of birth,** we take a solemn oath to attempt to be a Mensch throughout our lives.

Then, in the very first years of **our childhood Jewish education** (Shabbat 104a)[6], we are taught that the Alef-Bet book doesn't list apples, cats, and xylophones. There are no simple nouns in the Jewish text. To the contrary, the alphabet begins with statements of values to serve us as guides for our daily relationships with other people: "א-ב/Alef-Bet" stands for "אלף בינה/Elaf Bina, Learn wisdom." "Wisdom" is what we *do* with the facts we learn. "ג-ד/Gimel-Dalet" stands for "גמול דלים/Gemol Dalim, Take care of people in need." *That* is the wisdom that we ought to derive from our knowledge and intelligence.

Finally, in the Next World, **when we are asked to give an accounting for our lives,** we are asked, "What was your occupation?" In that text (Midrash on Psalms, 118:17)[7], the six correct answers are: (1) providing food for hungry people, (2) providing water for those who are thirsty, (3) providing clothes for people in need of clothing, (4) raising orphans, (5) using money for Mitzvahs (10-20%, Shulchan Aruch, Yoreh De'ah 249:1)[8], and (6) using our talents, brains, time, and effort to perform acts of caring, loving kindness. These 6 occupations can take many forms, such as: (1) Life-saver and Life-giver, (2) Dignity-restorer, (3) Everyday-miracle-worker, (4) Mitzvah-magician, (5) Hope-giver, (6) Dream-weaver, (7) Personifier-of-the-gentle-human-touch, (8) Solution-maker, (9) Tool-user-for-Mitzvahs, (10) Tool-maker-for-Mitzvahs, (11) Soul-repairer, (12) Broken-body-fixer, (13) Mitzvah-power-hungry-person, and (14) Part-time or full-time Creator-of-Mitzvah-radiance.

The Tzedakah/Mitzvah Continuum of Life

Parents realize very quickly that every child is different. Each individual child matures physically, intellectually, emotionally, and spiritually at varied real-time stages. In terms of Tzedakah and Mitzvahs, this means each parent will have to gauge on an individual basis when his or her child is ready to donate things he or she owns…and money. This includes that all-important moment when a child gives away items not only that he or she no longer needs or uses, but also those he or she *still* uses or needs. That realization — that others may need them more than they, themselves, do — is a critical step towards becoming a Mitzvah Person.

Bar/Bat Mitzvah Age

By Bat/Bar Mitzvah age, one meaningful way of preparing your child for entering Mitzvah Manhood and Womanhood would be to review his or her own personal history of giving things away. For example, you might say, *"Ziessa, Shayna* Miriam, do you remember when you were just 5 that you gave away your video of *101 Dalmations*, even though you used to watch it at least 7 times a day?" Remind your child that he or she, you yourselves, and other family members, already have a long history of giving. This may make it easier for the Bar/Bat Mitzvah to give away some of the inevitably-larger quantities of donatable items streaming in and whirling around at this stage of life.

Here is a *very* partial list of future times, beginning with the day after Bar/Bat Mitzvah ceremonies are over:

Post-Bar/Bat Mitzvah

The day before the Bar/Bat Mitzvah, parents should carefully consider what kinds of things to discuss with the Bar/Bat Mitzvah. Some parents might view this particular day like a pre-game pep talk from a coach in the locker room. Or they may relate to their child like a therapist evaluating their child's stress level. It will be valuable to take an hour or two to review the moment-by-moment "agenda" of the ceremony and its various rituals, including a brush-up of the texts the Glorious Child will be reciting. Others may choose to discuss a heavy philosophical overview of life, love, giving, and the pursuit of happiness, or a combination of some or all of these topics. Still other parents have found it beneficial to give their child the day off from school, according to the child's individual personal needs. Any of these possibilities may be appropriate, depending on the real needs of each specific family.

The Bar/Bat Mitzvah events themselves are described in the rest of this book. The remaining questions relate to the "post-" times…the day after, as everyone is "coming down" from the events; the week after; a year later, and other periodic times of reflection and action. Again, on these occasions it is important that parents and child take stock and articulate their feelings about the Bar/Bat Mitzvah.

It is certainly appropriate to be nostalgic, but, beyond that, it would be good to have a plan of action. For example, one insightful educator, Amy Ripps of Beth Mayer Synagogue in Raleigh, NC, has the 8th grade religious school class planning Mitzvah projects for the younger students in the schools.

Other possibilities include answers to questions like:

Will **the anniversary of the Bar/Bat Mitzvah** be remembered and marked on a calendar like a birthday?

On the anniversary of the Bar/Bat Mitzvah, will the child go with the family to synagogue and read the Torah portion and/or Haftarah?

Will the child re-visit his or her Mitzvah project, launch a new one, or, as in a few instances, keep his or her project going? After all, if it worked well once, why not continue to do it?

A wonderful example of the last scenario is Amy Sacks' "Amy's Holiday Party" in Atlanta. Amy wanted to throw a party for homeless children during the winter holiday season. It began in 1995 with 25 kids from shelters along with family members, on a budget of $400 Tzedakah money from her Bat Mitzvah. By the time she was a junior in college, her 9th Amy's Party had grown to 450 kids and families, with no indication of any annual Amy's Party being the last one. Amy's Party, of course, entails a huge time investment and fund-raising effort. (The 9th party cost $10,000.) But I repeat: There is no need to compare your own project to Amy's or to be intimidated by how awesome hers might be. Anything less is not a lesser Mitzvah. There is no such thing as a small Mitzvah, and *any* project a by post-Bat/Bar Mitzvah Mitzvah Woman or Mitzvah Man makes a *big* difference.

Additional Mitzvah Time-Line Possibilities

Many **high schools** have a community service requirement. The lessons of Bar/Bat Mitzvah should make it easy for this to be fulfilled with enthusiasm, and as deeds of pure, unadulterated Tikkun Olam. Later on, if The Glorious Child is going off to college and/or graduate school, parents still play an important role in their child's Life of Mitzvah. For example, they should make sure that their about-to-enter-college student *first* packs a Tzedakah box/*pushka,* even before putting in the laptop, DVD player, and other necessities (like clothes). They should be encouraged to seek out Tikkun Olam opportunities while at school…not only those offered by the university volunteer office, but also specifically *Jewish* ones. The same is true for Alternative Spring and Winter Break. They might consider putting in Mitzvah-time in Israel or in some *Jewish* project on this side of the ocean.

Getting married would include donating money to Tzedakah, having others donate money in honor of this magnificent event, having all the ceremonies and *things* associated with the event follow the patterns described for Bar/Bat Mitzvah. This would, of course, include living Jewishly with your spouse.

If there are children, the **baby naming** would include many of the items mentioned through this book, plus giving the miraculous newborn child a Jewish name that will carry great meaning throughout the person's life.

Significant birthdays: Mitzvah projects tied to these celebrations are often the best defense against pre-mid-life and mid-life crisis. For example, two of my good friends, Minna Heilpern and Judy Kupchan, asked their friends to donate in their honor towards purchasing a Mitzvah horse for the Israel National Therapeutic Riding Association (INTRA). The INTRA people purchased a gorgeous mare named Pocahontas. As it happened, Minna and Judy got a two-for-one Mitzvah. Pocahontas was pregnant, and the foal, now colt, now pony (named "Siegel," by the way), will become a future Mitzvah horse in her own right.

If a person is fortunate to experience the joys of being a **grandparent** or **great-grandparent,** those particular stages of life also offer multiple opportunities for Mitzvahs, Tzedakah, and Tikkun Olam unique to those years.

Finally, *way down the road,* to bring the time line full circle, at *Shiva* people would donate to Tzedakah in your memory. You could specify long ahead of time exactly where they should give the Mitzvah-money. From the עוֹלָם הבא/Olam HaBa, The Next World, you would enjoy listening to the warm, uplifting stories they are telling about your Life of Mitzvahs.

So Your Child Doesn't Talk to You ...

*O*r at best manages one- or two-word sentences or a grunt, mumbling string of incomprehensible syllables, hum, or other semi-sound. These might be a response to your questions about her or his wellbeing, schoolwork, friends, Sunday schedule, preparations for Bar/Bat Mitzvah, or precisely when she or he might be thinking of picking the clothes up from the floor.

Ask your child about what he or she considers "קדוש/Kadosh, holy" in his or her own life. If that particular word does not elicit a response, try words like "important," "meaningful," "valuable," "precious," "priceless," or similarly-loaded words. From there, you might proceed to asking why and how the Bar/Bat Mitzvah is important to them, why they want to do it, and what part of the entire event means the most to them.

This also might be a good time to review the facts and feelings about the events of your own Bar/Bat Mitzvah. If — for whatever reason — you did not have your own ceremony at the age-appropriate time, but instead celebrated an adult Bar/Bat Mitzvah, communicate to them as powerfully as you can why you decided to do it and the deep emotions you felt when it actually took place. I cannot stress this latter point enough. In my years of travel, I have never, I repeat, never, heard an adult Bar/Bat Mitzvah who was not profoundly moved by the experience. Many times adults describe this their personal experience in terms of "spiritual," "sublime," and "life-changing." I would think your child would benefit greatly from under-standing just how powerful an experience it was, and how it remains an active part of your Jewish consciousness.

Consider how different the content of this topic is from the stories you (hopefully jokingly) told them about how you used to have to walk to school uphill both ways, or that you were just too poor to own a cat or a dog, so all you had was a pet paper clip you named Silver Meteor. They were probably as attentive as when you recited what presents you got for your Bat/Bar Mitzvah — name bracelets, cufflinks, tie bars, travel alarm clocks with your initials embossed on them, and a half-dozen fountain pens. (You probably had to explain to them what a "fountain pen" was.)

I think it is worth a try. You may or may not succeed, but I definitely believe it is worth a try.

Bar/Bat Mitzvah of Individuals With "Special" Needs

A Historical Note

"Special" B'nai and B'not Mitzvah are no longer a rarity.

Not so very long ago, Bar/Bat Mitzvah events for individuals with special needs were relegated to out-of-the-way dates such as Shabbat Mincha/Saturday afternoon, or secular holiday Monday mornings like Labor Day or Memorial Day. Congregations (and camps, youth groups, family education programs, religious schools, and day schools) have increasing numbers of integrated programs. Programs such as Camp Ramah's Tikvah Programs have been around for more than 25 years; the Americans and Canadians with Disabilities Acts are an accepted fact in society that no one questions any more. Parents no longer need to search for additional tutors for their child. They have become available, not as if by magic, but because congregations understand "community" differently than they might have a couple of decades ago. Synagogues no longer feel that they are "accommodating." The Bar/Bat Mitzvah of an individual with special needs *just is,* like Yom Kippur *is,* or the reading of the Torah *just is* in the life of the congregation.

Definitions

No matter what vocabulary one uses, some people will be happy, and others will be offended. "Special" "exceptional" "challenged" — all are partially good descriptives, and yet all are inadequate. Many people particularly dislike the term "challenged," since the individual and his or her family and friends often feel more overwhelmed than "challenged."

In particular, "LD" as "learns differently" is problematic. For individuals like Samantha Abeel who has dyscalculia and can't tell time, count money, or do anything else with numbers or sequences, it is true that she learns differently. But the very real fact of her life is she has a serious learning disability that affects the way she functions every day. There is even a misapprehension that "LD" is a kind of "lightweight" special needs. This is also changing, but slowly. Progress is definitely apparent, but the effort to find the most appropriate terminology continues.

What we can say, though, is that whatever the term, what was once a rarity, i.e., Bat/Bar Mitzvah of people with special needs, is now a "normal" event nearly everywhere. And this includes B'not/B'nai Mitzvah of young people who have struggled with, are still fighting, or are in the process of overcoming the effects of a serious disease.

The Community's Experience, Things Learned

The most common word I hear when friends describe a Bat or Bar Mitzvah of someone with special needs is "moving." Parents, siblings, relatives, friends, and regular attendees at synagogue services are deeply moved by the events of the day. Tears flow freely. One reason, clearly, is a sense of pride in the Bat/Bar Mitzvah's achievement.

Beyond achievement, though, I believe are other elements. I think the congregants feel justifiably good that, in a sense, they have "grown up." They take pride in the fact that a "special" Simcha such as this is no longer so "special." Rather, it is just one more aspect of what makes the congregation a בית כנסת/Bet Knesset — an open, welcoming place for all of its members to gather and share Life's significant moments. There is nothing patronizing in their attitude. As individuals, couples, families grow, change, and mature, so do congregations and communities. The change may have taken more time than many congregants and leaders may have wanted, but it *has* happened and they feel a sense of joy that they have matured. In fact, the day has come in many communities where explaining that, "in the old days" there was no such event as a special needs Bar/Bat Mitzvah, is like telling young people that there was a time when cars didn't have seat belts. This is similar to their feeling that has been accepted practice that a Bar/Bat Mitzvah has to have a Mitzvah project. That's just the way things are at Temple Shalom or Tikvat Israel.

Beyond what is stated in the previous paragraph I think there is an additional element to consider. It is what my friend and teacher, Rabbi David Stern, says is the *authenticity* of what the congregation sees and hears. There is neither time nor need for people to focus on other, often-superficial aspects of some B'nai/B'not Mitzvah: fancy parties, how perfectly someone recited his or her Torah portion and how typical it is of a super-achiever to do it perfectly. Indeed, the special needs Bat/Bar Mitzvah provides a time to reflect on more profound values, what *really* is important about people as people, whether they have special needs or not. Of course, people often *do* reflect on these issues, such as when they support Make a Wish Foundation or read an article about The Special Olympics. But this may be a first time for many to think about everything in a *Jewish* context. It allows them to refine their understanding of words like "normal," "special," "gifted," and "talented." IQ as a supreme criterion-of-value is, for many, being replaced by "CQ," Caring Quotient.

A recent story I heard may help us all work through this in our own thinking: The director of a Jewish camp noticed that, during that period of time when campers with special needs were present for one session, the other campers were fabulously sensitive and had no trouble inter-relating and acting naturally. What troubled him was that, when the special needs campers left, the "normal" campers often slid back into some of their nasty habits of treating each other not-so-nicely. The spill-over of sensitivity and more authentic values of caring was not as forceful as he, the counselors, and other staff would have wanted. This, too, will change, with time. Let us hope it will be sooner rather than later, but it will happen. As I once wrote when I imagined a Bar Mitzvah speech by an individual with special needs:

I need *you*; *you* need *me*.
If I am out, you are no-one;
in, we are The People God chose when He chose Abraham,
all Jews.
No one is special.
Everyone is special.

Postscript — On Being a Little Einstein

In the past few years, the phrase "a person with special needs" has become a much more sensitive description than "a person with disabilities." There is no question that a person who is so visually impaired he or she cannot drive has a disability. The same is true for someone who uses a wheelchair, no matter how well he or she negotiates sidewalks that do not have curb cuts or entrances to buildings that have steps but no ramp. "Special needs," on the other hand, allows all of us to hear the word "needs," and to respond by taking care of those needs in any way our creativity and budgets will allow. This is verbal progress which leads to Tikkun Olam.

As a term, "special" is far from perfect. Indeed, many consider it to be patronizing. Still, using this word shows that language is slowly beginning to catch up to the reality of human needs and sensitivities. It is a good, but not sufficient, step in the right direction.

Furthermore, there is a positive aspect of "special" needs that, in my opinion, has not been stressed sufficiently — that the disability, whatever it is, may, indeed, be the *source* of an exceptional talent waiting to be developed. The story of Albert Einstein, who changed the way we look at the universe, is a classic and wonderful example:

A couple of generations ago, one of the highest compliments someone could give a parent was to say, "Your child is a little Einstein." That person was referring to how intellectually bright the child was. Later on, people became aware of the fact that when Einstein was a student in school, he performed poorly in elementary mathematics. *That* was an important revelation for many people. Still, there is one more level of meaning to this part of Einstein's biography, something very deep and insightful. As he expressed it in his own words,

"When I ask myself how it happened that I in particular discovered the

Relativity Theory, it seemed to lie in the following circumstance. The normal adult never bothers his head about space-time problems. Everything there is to be thought about, in his opinion, has already been done in early childhood. I, on the contrary, developed so slowly that I only began to wonder about space and time when I was already grown up. In consequence, I probed deeper into the problem than an ordinary child would have done."

So the great man himself came to realize that his particular disability was the very source of his greatest breakthrough! While we may not expect such an enormous impact on humanity from others — Einstein was One in a Century — surely this insight is worth exploring at greater length with every individual with special needs. It may be that we have overlooked something because we concentrated too much on *dis*-ability. Perhaps we should look at the inability to do *some* things as the very wellspring of enormous talents for innovation and invention.

For Einstein, it was physics.

For others, it may be Mitzvahs and Tikkun Olam.

Everything Relating

To the Event Itself and

All Those Additional Events

Associated With

The Big Event

Invitations, Mitzvah-Centerpieces, Mitzvah- and Double-Mitzvah -Challahs and -Challah Covers

שמעון בנו אומר...
ולא המדרש הוא העקר אלא המעשה

Shimon [the son of Rabban Gamliel] says:
It is not what one says, but rather what one does,
that makes all the difference in the world. *(Pirke Avot 1:17)*

There are so many *things* associated with the events of a Bat or Bar Mitzvah. For any Simcha of this nature, the person in charge has a list of *"things* to take care of." These may include "Remember to pick up Uncle Max at the airport, United 227, at 4:38" and "Double-check to make sure they rolled the Torah to the right place so My Glorious Child won't get rattled." This chapter deals with several *tangible things,* almost all of which have Mitzvah-potential. It is my belief that almost any *thing* can become a Mitzvah-*thing*. What follows are some examples of how many items relating to Bar/Bat Mitzvah, often taken for granted as "ordinary" can be transformed into Mitzvah-objects and articles, endowed by the family with their full Mitzvah-power.

The Invitation

To connect yourself with the thousands of years of the history of the Jewish people, you will want to use Hebrew names, words, and phrases alongside the English. This is a *Jewish* event. This is *our* language, and this gives you a chance to be good teachers to many people who might otherwise be unfamiliar with the most important concepts, values, and terms in Jewish life. In addition to the invitation, you have other opportunities to make Hebrew a part of the Bar/Bat Mitzvah event, such as an explanatory hand-out sheet given to congregants and guests when they enter the sanctuary for services. A basic vocabulary list of essential words in Hebrew, translation, and transliteration is a useful aid for those people who might be unfamiliar with Hebrew. One additional item: If the Bar/Bat Mitzvah has produced flyers or brochures about his or her project, there, too, Hebrew vocabulary is appropriate.

You may wish to join the growing trend to "downspend" on the expenditure for the invitation. This means that whatever you had planned to budget for invitations, go down a level or two or three and donate the difference to Tzedakah. Do this *in honor of your child.* In fact, what you will be doing is *upgrading* in Mitzvahs. By telling your daughter or son what you are doing and why you are doing it, you are sending a very powerful message and reinforcing your position as a role model for your child. This is particularly critical at a time such as Bar/Bat Mitzvah. Tell them that you are going to pass on Lucite, videotape or DVD invitations, and invitations that cost $2.44 to mail, and that the money you are saving you are donating in their honor to fix the world. This is a wonderful lesson about Jewish values that you will be teaching your daughter or son.

The challenging part is explaining that at certain times in life you have to take a stand against social pressures. To your son or daughter, the issue of invitations may not seem so important. However, the discussion may still be particularly difficult since, during this same period of time, they are receiving more elaborate invitations from their classmates and peers. This may not be an easy task, but, in my opinion, it is definitely worthwhile. However your child reacts, he or she will always remember having had the discussion. As an "adult," he or she will refer back to it at different times in life when similar decisions have to be made about "for me" and "for others."

You may even go so far as to suggest that the Bar/Bat Mitzvah and family use its computer graphic skills to design the format and text. It will allow your child a much more active part to best express *his or her* grasp of the meaning of Bat/Bar Mitzvah.

In a growing number of B'nai and B'not Mitzvah invitations, there is a Mitzvah-insert in the envelope. This is the card or letter your son or daughter writes about his or her Mitzvah project. I have frequently learned of incredible responses to the Mitzvah project because this document is written in his or her own words. Check the punctuation and grammar, of course — and (I say politely) re-check your own — but let the words flow from your child's own נשמה/Neshama, soul. Expressions like "It would make me very happy if you would bring gently-used kid videotapes to the reception on מוצאי שבת/Motza'ay Shabbat, Saturday night. These tapes will be donated to...," and "At this very important time in my Jewish life, I realize how fortunate I am. I am therefore asking you to join me in the Mitzvah of..." are just two of many beautiful expressions of a Bar/Bat Mitzvah growing up Jewish. And if, just if, your child is not eloquent or even barely articulate, nevertheless, a C-grade composition on this insert is incredibly more powerful than any stock or unnatural phraseology in a printer's invitation manual could ever be, because it is authentic.

And there is even one more step in this personalization process. Whether the invitation is done "professionally" or on a home computer, it is now relatively simple to reproduce the message in your child's own handwriting. It's much more personal and meaningful and *definitely* more powerful. I believe it would be very difficult for others to resist joining your child in her or his chosen Tikkun Olam if the invitees received such a personalized invitation.

The Centerpieces (and Bima Arrangements)

Flowers

To have flowers or not to have flowers, that is the question.

Flowers *per se,* to quote the poet, are "a thing of beauty." If you do decide to have flowers (or plants) as centerpieces, there are several ways to connect them to Mitzvahs. Above all else, as with the invitations, consider "downspending" from your original plan and donating the difference to Tzedakah in your child's honor. The second, and obvious, way is to donate the centerpieces after the events are over. They can make many people very happy…in institutions such as hospitals, nursing homes, or shelters. You may even want to give them to individuals living alone who might very well need some extra element of pure, simple beauty in their lives. Your rabbi, other congregants, friends, social workers, and social service agencies will be good resources for identifying individuals who would derive great pleasure from receiving the flowers.

You may feel a little uncertain about this particular Mitzvah, particularly **if you are not "a flower person."** There is a relatively simple solution: Find a florist who is an expert on Mitzvah centerpieces, or at least one who will listen sympathetically and carefully to what you want to accomplish. I recently learned many facts from my old friend, Rabbi Chaim Casper, who owns a flower shop in Miami Beach, Florida. In 10 minutes he taught me about several kinds of plants — some types or bromeliads, for example — that would be especially appropriate to give to residents of nursing homes. They are easy to care for, flower beautifully, and grow at a quick pace that is satisfying to the person taking care of the plant. When I asked about breaking up a big centerpiece to give to individuals, he assured me that it is relatively easy to make one composed of flowers in *individual* vases. He suggested orchids and/or roses as possible choices. In our short conversation, he offered many other suggestions which I never would have thought possible. Again, the solution is to find the right florist[9].

Delivering the flowers or plants: Best of all, of course, is delivering the flowers or plants as a family. Your child should be an integral part of this experience and should have the joy of saying something like, "I just became a Bar/Bat Mitzvah. I wanted to share the goodness, beauty, and happiness of this moment with you." As a parent, you are offering your daughter or son an opportunity which could become one of the unforgettable memories long into their adulthood. I personally believe that a significant part of a parent's (and teacher's) "job" is to be, as it were, Unforgettable Memory Providers…and some of those memories clearly should be Mitzvah-memories. As a part of this memory building, you may have your child design and compose the card for the center of the table which will explain that the flowers are being donated.

In addition to all the glories of the above flower Mitzvahs, you can purchase flowers grown in Israel. You can also purchase vases from Israeli artists and merchants, and include this information on the card mentioned above. www.whiteplainsforisrael.org, the website of the Five Synagogues Israel Action Committee (of White Plains, NY) gives you more than a dozen places from whom to order flowers from Israel.

A Recent Trend: Centerpieces Other Than Flowers

It is definitely much more acceptable nowadays to have centerpieces that do not involve flowers. Every week I hear of more Bar/Bat Mitzvah families choosing an ever-growing variety of items used as centerpieces and Bima arrangements that can be donated to various agencies, organizations and individuals. This is just one more aspect of Mitzvahs and Tikkun Olam that has taken hold of the Great Event.

Just a few of the items that are now being used include: canned, boxed, and jarred food, toys, books, games, puzzles, sports equipment, shoes, stuffed animals and dolls, baby items, toiletries, cosmetics, videotapes, CDs and DVDs, balloons, plants, gloves, warm hats, and scarves. One Bar Mitzvah "got it" about sports equipment because he knows how expensive hockey equipment is. Every time he suited up, he realized it would be impossible for many others to afford these necessities. *Something* had to be done, and he was the one who was going to make this piece of Tikkun Olam happen.

If this limited list doesn't particularly move you, *thinking Mitzvahs* with family and friends for a half hour should certainly produce just the right Mitzvah-centerpiece and/or Bima arrangement you are looking for.

Several families feature different Mitzvah projects as centerpieces. At each table is a brief summary of the kind of Tikkun Olam work the project does, occasionally with a display of brochures available for guests to take with them. A lovely variation on this idea is featuring Mitzvah heroes. I have heard of B'not/B'nai Mitzvah using photographs and descriptions of the lives of these great people. In fact, we were recently consulted by a future Bat Mitzvah and her family. She wanted to feature great Jewish women and was very enthusiastic to learn of our many women Mitzvah heroes. By a stroke of good timing, she even had the opportunity to speak to one of them — Anita Shkedi, founder of the Israeli National Therapeutic Riding Association — for more than an hour by phone. She will be one of the featured women Mitzvah heroes on the Bat Mitzvah's tables.

Finally, if you keep Israel in mind at every stage of the Bar/Bat Mitzvah planning, it becomes easy to consider that some of these items can be donated to appropriate organizations, institutions, or individuals in Israel. Finding the right place to donate is not too difficult. **Start with www.ziv.org.**

The *only* — I repeat — the *only* problem with donating to individuals in Israel is the *shlepping*...you know, finding a way to actually get the

Mitzvah-goods to Israel. There are a number of solutions: If a family trip to Israel is a vital aspect of your Bat/Bar Mitzvah event, you have solved the problem. If not, then you should look for individuals or local groups going over who would be willing to take them for you. Remind them that these are Mitzvah-items from your Bat/Bar Mitzvah, and that they are thereby becoming your שליח/Shaliach, Mitzvah Messenger. This will offer them an additional sacred element to their tour of Israel.

The Mitzvah centerpiece movement is just one more aspect of the difficult struggle that transforms the over-emphasis on the child's ego to the child-as-giver. It is hoped that when a family considers the options listed above, at least some of them will re-think the need for centerpieces that feature themes such as the ones that stress luaus, retro 70's, or movie stars.

Tablecloths

There are at least two options for tying in Mitzvahs to the tablecloths you choose to use. Again, keeping Israel always in mind, you can purchase them from Israeli merchants. Another possibility is if you happen to have a family heirloom tablecloth. You may have one embroidered by an ancestor and handed down from generation to generation. What more appropriate time place to make use of it that at the Bat/Bar Mitzvah? This further enhances the sense of Jewish continuity which is ever-so-important at a time like this in your family's and the community's life-experience.

The Explanatory Card

Near the centerpiece and in front of the Bima displays should be a nicely-decorated, clearly-stated card explaining exactly where the items will be donated. Be sure to include any contact information. If they were purchased as Mitzvah-items, this, too, should be included in the message. It may be that some of the guests will be inspired by this Mitzvah-act and will themselves want to do more for the various beneficiaries.

Some families choose to donate to Tzedakah in honor of their friends, relatives and other guests. An appropriately-worded card to that effect should also be placed at the center of the table. It should explain how happy and honored the family is that you have come to the Simcha, and that this is the best way they could think of to thank you and honor you. As with the invitation, the Bar/Bat Mitzvah himself or herself should provide the text for the card in his or her own words, and, if possible, reproduced in the Bar/Bat Mitzvah's own handwriting.

The Hand Washing Cup

This ritual item may also be purchased from Israeli Mitzvah projects or merchants.

The חלות/Challot

At many Jewish celebrations, we have become used to the presence of a humongous 20-pound Challah. After the המוציא/HaMotzi blessing is recited, it mysteriously disappears, whisked away into some black hole behind swinging doors leading to the kitchen. It reappears, sliced all nicely and neatly by some unknown individual, and small pieces are then distributed to the guests.

Since this is a סעודת מצוה/Se'udat Mitzvah, Mitzvah meal, we should step back for a moment in order to begin the process of "Mitzvah-izing" this aspect of the Bar/Bat Mitzvah. First of all, the Bar/Bat Mitzvah and family may want to actually bake the Challot. It may be the Glorious Kid's first opportunity to experience this extremely hands-on type of Mitzvah...and do not be surprised if your *son* actually *loves* to do it. The sexism of Challah-baking is a thing of the past. You may also want to replicate a wonderful Mitzvah project started by Dr. Michael Nissenblatt in New Jersey. He supplies the funds for his patients and former patients to make the rounds at a local hospital to distribute Challot on Friday afternoons to Jewish people who will be spending Shabbat there. You could ask the Rabbi for a list of Jewish patients presently in the hospital. Whether you, yourselves, are baking or if you are buying, you can make or buy extras and help make their Shabbat in the hospital a little more tolerable.

I mention another recently-seen custom in some synagogues. There are two schools of thought on how the Challah is to be divided — "cutters" and "tearers." You might want to be a "tearer." Have the family members surround the Challah when you make the blessing, and have every person puts his or her hand on the Challah. Then everyone tears off a piece. The remaining large portion can be torn and then distributed to the other guests. This method has a bit more of a *haimisch*/hospitable touch to it.

The Challah Covers

These may be purchased from merchants or Mitzvah projects in Israel, or from Mitzvah projects in the United States or Canada. Wonderful variations are to have them made specially by family members or friends who might want to do it to be a more active part of the celebration. In some communities, you can organize a project to have Elders in the local nursing home or assisted living make them. Inviting the Elders to the celebration would certainly be a double Mitzvah: הכנסת אורחים/Hachnassat Orchim, Hospitality and, second, הידור פני זקן/Hiddur P'nai Zaken, Bringing Out the Radiance in the Faces of Our Elders.

To summarize, at almost every turn, there are so many opportunities for "Mitzvah-izing." To whatever extent you choose to change the mundane to the more sublime, the benefits to the Bar/Bat Mitzvah and everyone else who join you will be very great.

Yarmulkas/Kippot, The Tallit, Tallit Bag, And Other Ritual Items: Double-Mitzvah Opportunities

Candlesticks, Kiddush cups, Challah covers, טליתות/Tallitot, כיפות/kippot (yarmulkas), a יד/Yad/pointer for reading from the Torah — ritual objects are everywhere to be seen during the course of The Big Event. Each one is an item that serves a Mitzvah purpose. So many Mitzvahs are available at a Bat/Bar Mitzvah! So much variety, so many opportunities. This is definitely a cause for celebration. But there is reason for even more pleasure — a doubling of the Mitzvah, as it were, because all of these items may be purchased from Mitzvah projects. So besides having the Mitzvah-items themselves, your family can be supporting some incredible Tikkun Olam work.

A stunning example is buying כיפות/kippot (yarmulkas). Guatemalan Mayan woman are now crocheting the most gorgeous, multi-colored kippot that have been selling so quickly that the women think that everyone in North America is Jewish! If you are tired of opening that drawer at home with two dozen standard kippot inscribed in gold letters, "Charlene's (Tricia's, Cheyenne's, Missy's, Morgan's, Brandy's, Draysha Frimma's, Liora's, Li-at's, Li-Lach's, Li'tal's, Meital's, Tali's) Bat/Bar Mitzvah" — this is absolutely the best way to prevent spreading the plague-of-unwanted-kippot to friends and relatives. The project that produces the kippot is called MayaWorks, and the yarmulkas have become so popular, you will need to order well ahead of time. [www.mayaworks.org.] This is a superb example of Maimonides' highest level of Tzedakah, which states "…giving that person a gift, or a loan, or becoming a partner, or finding a job for that person, to strengthen the person's hand, so that the person can become self-supporting…." The money that the Mayan women earn puts food on the table and provides for other Life-necessities for themselves and their families.

Ethiopian Jews produce gorgeous טליתות/Tallitot and Tallit Bags under the aegis of The North American Conference on Ethiopian Jewry (NACOEJ). [www.nacoej.org] The Tallit bags come in a wide variety of Biblical and Ethiopian designs: Daniel in the Lion's Den, Jonah and the Whale, the Kes (Ethiopian spiritual leader) teaching students, The Queen of Sheba. The designs — in dazzling colors — are simply gorgeous. A more recent product are the טליתות/Tallitot produced by Ethiopian Jews still in Addis Ababa, awaiting their turn to make Aliya to Israel. They are woven in two ranges of bright colors, in both larger and smaller sizes. I purchased one in the summer of 2003, and whenever I am in synagogues for my lectures, several people approach and ask where they can get one for themselves.

A note concerning the purchase of תְּפִילִין/Tfillin: They can be expensive, and even very expensive. To know what is kosher or not kosher in a particular set of Tfillin, you need great expertise. The most reliable way to buy Tfillin is to ask a person you trust to provide the contact information for someone who can explain everything simply and fairly. For this purchase, you need an expert who knows your needs no less than when you are buying a new computer.

Several ritual items such as candlesticks, Kiddush Cups, a יָד/Yad, pointer for reading from the Torah can also become a double-Mitzvah. Some congregations give the Bar/Bat Mitzvah one or more of these items. The double-Mitzvah is this: They are themselves Mitzvah-objects, and these particular items are now being produced at בית חם/Bayit Cham in B'nai B'rak, Israel. Bayit Cham, founded by two most exceptional people, Shmuel Munk and Yoram Mordechai, find employment opportunities for individuals who are recovering from severe mental and emotional distress. The work that they engage in is a significant aspect of their total rehabilitation. Among those Shmuel and Yoram have worked with is a silversmith who fashions these beautiful items. Purchasing these ritual objects from Bayit Cham is absolutely a double Mitzvah. [baitcham@zahav.net.il]

If you as a family are considering giving a gift to the congregation, this silversmith has also created many suitable articles from which to choose such as Menorahs and Mezuzzot. In addition, you may wish to encourage your synagogue to give a Yad or Kiddush cup to each Bar/Bat Mitzvah and also to have your synagogue gift shop sell these items. By any of these methods, you will be making very real Maimonides' highest level of Tzedakah.

How I Feel When I Hold My Great-Grandmother's Shabbat Candlesticks In My Hands

In some families, the Bar/Bat Mitzvah may be particularly fortunate. Besides the new ritual items they get at this all-important moment, they may receive family heirlooms such as a great-grandparent's Kiddush cup or Shabbat candlesticks. These are priceless. I don't mean that if they were stolen, you would have to tell the insurance company that they had "great sentimental value." This is neither about "sentimental value" nor "symbolic meaning." The heirlooms are much more — they are authentic items, touchable, usable for ritual. They are not merely "symbolic" of Jewish continuity. To the contrary, if they are used by the Bar/Bat Mitzvah the week after the event, they are Jewish continuity.

If the Bar/Bat Mitzvah is fortunate to receive one or more of the ritual items that were brought from The Old Country, so much greater the importance. This is why these particular gifts are priceless: When they hold them in their hands and set them on the table for blessing the candles or the wine, they will be reminded that Jews didn't appear as if by magic in North America, or that "they have been here forever." These immigrant ancestors came, in almost all cases, because they were fleeing danger and were in pursuit of freedom. When they were alive, they were alive and free. The family would do well to tell the "story" of these objects: who owned them, how they came to these shores, how they were passed on from one generation to the next, and, most of all, why they are being given to the Bat/Bar Mitzvah. With this historical perspective, the next generation should have a sense that "alive and free" really means "alive and free and Jewish."

Pushkas/Tzedakah Boxes

Finally, certainly one of my favorite ritual items — Tzedakah boxes. Many artisans and Mitzvah projects in Israel produce beautiful Tzedakah boxes. Here's where web surfing comes in: Have your child research various possibilities, and then jointly decide about the one he or she likes best. On a personal note, I believe it is a contradiction in terms to spend hundreds of dollars on a Tzedakah box, no matter how beautiful, no matter how wealthy the purchaser. Call me old fashioned. It's just the way I am. Use some good old time שׂכל/sechel, common sense when you purchase this particular item. The money saved can be put to better use for Tikkun Olam.

The Food

ood can be an integral Mitzvah component of the Simcha. A prime example deals with **the projected cost of the food.** Whatever you may have planned to budget for the various events relating to the Bar/Bat Mitzvah, you may wish to consider that less-than-expensive menus are just as acceptable. I personally enjoy dim sum, nigiri sushi, and empanadas and can gobble them with the best of noshers, but these are best left for other, less public occasions. Indeed, over the past four decades, I have been in more than 500 congregations, and I have been pleasantly surprised that in some of the most upscale synagogues, there are strict rules that allow for only modest spreads. You may decide that what applies in the synagogue is also appropriate for meals served in your home or other locations where you are feeding your guests. In any event, beyond the suggestions listed below, consider the possibility of looking at what you had budgeted, then "downspend" a level or two. Donate the money you saved to Tzedakah. Your daughter or son will have already begun the "Bat/Bar Mitzvah Circuit" and will have a good idea of what is appropriate, or too little, or considerably beyond the norm.

One of my friends suggested the following analogy concerning money spent on Bar and Bat Mitzvah events. He said that it is similar to the way some people look at vacation money. They don't worry about or haggle if the gondola ride is $13 or $15 per person. I find the image very useful when considering how much to spend "on us" and "for the benefit of other people." Of course, as you are making these plans, it would be good to discuss them with your child, so that he or she will get a better sense of what is appropriate to spend "on us," and — from the Tzedakah side — for the benefit of other people. Tell your child you are donating the difference to Tzedakah *in his or her honor,* and jointly decide where this Tzedakah money will make the most impact on the lives of people in need.

The most common issue is, of course, **donating leftover food.** For many B'nai and B'not Mitzvah, there will be several occasions to serve food: at the synagogue or wherever the ceremony is being held, and at your home. It would be most appropriate to donate leftover food to individuals who otherwise would not have enough to eat. From the earliest days of your preparations for the Bar/Bat Mitzvah, explain to your child that you are donating leftover food, and why it is so important to you to make this Mitzvah an integral part of the celebration. You may also want to explain that in some communities, the sheer quantities of food that continue to be thrown out every week at B'nai and B'not Mitzvah events is shameful. In Jewish tradition, donating food involves a positive and a negative Mitzvah. Negative: תשחית בל/Bal Tashchit, not wasting food, and positive: רעבים האכלת/Ha'achalat Re'ayvim, feeding hungry people. Donating leftover food sets a fine example to other parents, members of the congregation, friends, and family. Parents, this certainly leaves a lasting impression on your child.

For those who are willing, the critical question naturally is how do you *actually* do it? The answers are easier than most would expect.

A frequently-asked question is, "Is it legal to donate?" The answer is a most emphatic "Yes!" The federal law known as the "Bill Emerson Good Samaritan Food Donation Act" clearly states that a good-faith donor is protected from liability. Here is the essential paragraph of the law:

Liability of person or gleaner.

A person or gleaner shall not* *be subject to civil or criminal liability arising from the nature, age, packaging, or condition of apparently whole-some food or an apparently fit grocery product that the person or gleaner donates in good faith to a non-profit organization for ultimate distribution to needy individuals. [*my emphasis]*

In the endnotes, I have provided an additional document — a legal form which is often signed between the caterer and those who are hiring the caterer[10].

Exactly *how* do you make the specific arrangements? If you are having a **caterer** provide some of the meals, your contract should clearly state that leftover food (all of it, or a portion that you designate) is to be donated to appropriate agencies. Caterers who do this regularly, know where to bring the food. If yours is not yet familiar with the options, this is an excellent opportunity to teach. You should add that donating leftover food is being done everywhere — in hotels, restaurants, university food services, and public and private schools, to name only a few venues. After you explain your desire to donate, if the caterer does not agree to the terms — *find another caterer.* We would hope it would not reach that point, but sometimes it does.

For food provided by other sources, the above section explains the legal details. If your synagogue has its own committee or you are preparing the food yourself, the most important next step is to locate an appropriate agency to receive the food. It is best to do your research well ahead of time. Meet with the group that provides for people in need and explain the kinds of food you would like to donate. Those agencies will help you understand which items may be legally donated. Much depends on the way the food was served, the needs of the agency, and the people they are feeding. The actual procedures are *not* as complicated as you might think. It should take no more than 15 minutes to learn the basic rules.

Once the meals are over and the food to be donated is assembled and packaged, **it needs to be delivered.** Some agencies pick up food, which solves the problem easily. If they do not, and the food actually needs to be delivered, ideally, the Bar/Bat Mitzvah and family members themselves can deliver it. This is just one more way to bring home the message that, while there are many aspects of Bar/Bat Mitzvah that are symbolic, Mitzvah-food is very, very real, and feeds bodies, minds, and souls of people who, for whatever reasons, do not have the ability to provide it for themselves.

You never really get a full sense of the quantity of food donated until you actually lift the trays and put them into the car to drive to the local meals-on-wheels program or soup kitchen. Twice I have had the opportunity to participate in this Mitzvah with my friends, the Engeharts of Chicago and the Goulds of Toronto. In neither case was it a bang-up overly-done gourmet affair, and yet, I can still feel the weight of the food years later. The *feeling* of the Mitzvah stays with you and comes back, even before it reaches the memory cells in the brain.

An additional important consideration concerns the hard-working people who set up and serve the food. It would be important to arrange with the caterer or others providing the food that **the waitstaff be allowed to eat *before* they serve.** I believe this is a most Menschlich Mitzvah-idea, and it is based on solid Jewish tradition hundreds of years old, back to the time of the Talmud (Ketubot 61a; Shulchan Aruch, Orach Chaim 169:1[11])

In addition to the above-mentioned Mitzvahs, there are several other possibilities concerning food. One, suggested by my friend and teacher, Sharon Halper, is **donating to a worthy Mitzvah hero or Tzedakah organization that feeds hungry people.** For example, the North American Conference on Ethiopian Jews (NACOEJ), has been able to supply a nutritious meal for Ethiopian Jewish children still waiting in Ethiopia to leave for Israel — for 25 cents a meal. She designed a simple sticker that says, "I am not eating alone," which can be attached to the place card or table seating card that explains that a donation has been made to provide food for these children. I think it is a very powerful idea, and can be done with many other variations.

More: You may choose to use as many Israeli food items as possible. Or — as some people are doing — explain to your friends and relatives that you are not having a party, but using the money instead to **take the family to Israel.** Still others have simultaneously paid for a festive meal, locally or in Israel, for people who might not be able to afford a lovely meal. It is a beautiful way to share the occasion, despite the great distances.

There are others who decide to throw **a pizza or schwarma party for Israeli soldiers,** complete with personal notes to the soldiers from the Bar/Bat Mitzvah, family, friends, and anyone else invited to the event. Stefanie Lopatkin of Great Neck, NY, decided to sponsor one of these parties while I was in Israel. It is difficult to put into words how much the soldiers appreciate the fun food. But even more, we hear from the soldiers that the personal notes from people far away who care about them and who write to them that they are not alone — these notes are what really gives them good feelings. Go to **www.ziv.org** for details on how to make this wonderful experience happen. 100% of your donation is used for the party.

Finally, according to Jewish tradition, this is a סעודת מצוה/**Se'udat Mitzvah, Mitzvah Meal.** Meals associated with the Bat/Bar Mitzvah are considered Mitzvah Meals, the same as any other food associated with a Jewish life-event. A דבר תורה/Dvar Torah is appropriate, i.e, a 5-minute Jewish-values talk using a traditional Jewish text. While you may invite the Rabbi or one of your Torah teachers to deliver the Dvar Torah, you may wish to invite some relative or honored guest, or — parents — you may decide to do it yourself. If it is your first-one-ever, so much the better. It is a wonderful experience, and one of the best role-model experiences you could provide for your child on this Great Day. It demonstrates unmistakably that Eema/Abba take Torah very seriously.

Now, as my ancestors used to say in Yiddish, "עם געזונט/Ess gezunt – You should eat in good health!"

The Speeches

בְּפִקֻּדֶיךָ אָשִׂיחָה וְאַבִּיטָה אֹרְחֹתֶיךָ:

**By talking about Your Mitzvahs,
I see more clearly the way You would like things to be.** *(Psalm 119:15)*

1. The Speech Delivered By The Glorious Kid — Some Things to Keep in Mind

The congregation is listening to you: your parents, other relatives, friends, parents' friends, congregants, your rabbi...and many of your teachers. Because this is such a special day, they may be paying more attention to what you have to say than what the Rabbi teaches every week. For those magic moments, you are the teacher. Besides teaching some Torah relating to your Torah reading or Haftarah and thanking those who have helped you along the way, this is a golden opportunity for you to tell them about your Mitzvah project.

You should understand that describing your Mitzvah project with enthusiasm is *not* bragging. You are educating others about ways to do Tikkun Olam, and Jewish tradition teaches us that לשם חינוך/Leshaym Chinuch, for the benefit of educating people, you are not only *allowed* to do it, you *should* do it, so others will do the same. In fact, encourage others to do as you are doing. As the Talmud teaches us *(Bava Batra 9a)*,

א"ר אלעזר גדול המעשה יותר מן העושה

Rabbi Elazar said: One who works to get others to give
is greater than one who only gives himself or herself.

You have *power* when you are speaking, even if you think you are not a good speaker. They will listen.

And keep in mind what your science teacher may have taught you — if a butterfly flutters its wings in some remote South American rain forest, it can change the weather as far away as Nebraska. So, too, with Mitzvahs. Any Mitzvah, no matter how ostensibly small, changes the entire world in so many ways you can barely begin to imagine the effects.

And to help you as you embark upon this journey of writing your speech, I have included a chapter with 85 useful quotes about Mitzvahs and Tikkun Olam.

2. The Speech Delivered By the Parent(s) of The Glorious Kid — Things to Keep in Mind

In some congregations, it is the custom for the parent(s) to address the child on the Bima. When presented tastefully and when deep sincerity breaks through the formality, when the delivery is not stilted, the speech(es) can be an exceptionally moving experience not only for the parents and the Bar/Bat Mitzvah, but also for the assembled congregation.

Remember, as with your child's speech, *they* are listening to you — your child, your parents, other relatives, friends, child's friends, yours and your child's teachers, and the many assembled congregants.

Tell your child how much you have been moved by her or his words and deeds, and how being proud on this day is *a different kind of* "proud" than taking pride in school, sports, and other activities. By speaking in this manner, you are setting an example for others to do the same, and at the same time reinforcing the higher significance of Bar/Bat Mitzvah.

Using a Jewish text as a point of departure not only gives you the opportunity to teach Torah to your child and to the congregation, it shows your child that Torah is very important to you on this Most Important Day. Role model seminars are everywhere. You don't need to spend $1,000 to learn how to be a role model on this day. Teach your child and the congregation some sweet Torah. You may also find it meaningful to speak of a personal hero, i.e. Mitzvah hero, in your own life. He or she may be a relative who inspired and continues to inspire you to do Mitzvahs. Tell your child that he or she is carrying on this Jewish tradition of a Life of Mitzvahs into a new generation, and *that* makes you very proud.

For these reasons, this is an especially appropriate time for you to recite the "שהחינו/Shehecheyanu" blessing. This is a *public* declaration that you thank The Holy One for giving you Life and allowing you to reach this most significant moment. Before you recite the blessing, you may want to tell the congregation that they should recite "Amen" with enthusiasm so that everyone present may feel the holiness of the moment.

Some Additional Ceremonies And Rituals

Some congregations around North America have introduced several interesting ways to make the Bar/Bat Mitzvah a more significant religious event. I believe that, despite the dangers of standardization and the occasional artificial "feel" of these moments, each has the *potential* to add an element more meaningful for the Bar/Bat Mitzvah, family, friends, and congregants. Five of them come to mind:

1. At the morning Minyan/service the Thursday before the Bar/Bat Mitzvah, the parents and siblings join the Bar/Bat Mitzvah for the ritual of putting on Tfillin. The Bar/Bat Mitzvah may lead part of the service and read from the Torah. This is an excellent reminder that prayer is not only a Shabbat or holiday experience, but happens daily.

2. In the early part of the Shabbat morning service, the parents present the Tallit to the Bar/Bat Mitzvah in the presence of the entire congregation. The Bat/Bar Mitzvah recites the blessing, and the entire congregation gets to respond "Amen." This young Jew, who is now officially joining the community as a full participant, learns once again that beyond family, there is Community with a capital "C." The message should come through very clearly: No one is ever alone and no one ever needs to feel alone.

3. When the Torah is taken out of the Ark, the family hands it over, starting with the earliest generation: great-grandparents, to grandparents, to parents and on to the New Generation. I would add that there should be a place for the Bar/Bat Mitzvah's teacher to be somewhere in the line, to stress once again how, beyond the basic biological history of our people, Torah constitutes a critical essence of our Jewish lives.

4. When the rabbi blesses the Bat/Bar Mitzvah, the parents join by placing their hands on her or his head and recite the blessing at the same time.

5. Rabbi Arthur Zuckerman, formerly of Congregation Beth Am in San Diego, would remove the original צִיצִית/Tzitzit, ritual fringes from the future Bar/Bat Mitzvah's new Tallit, and would hand the family

members a new set, including one blue thread. (Numbers 15:38) He then teaches them how to tie the Tzitzit to the cloth, and, together as a family, they would do the actual tying of the new threads. This is particularly powerful considering that, technically speaking, the cloth is secondary to the Tzitzit. The cloth itself is simply called the "בֶגֶד/Beged," which means no more than "a cloth, a piece of clothing." Now there is an important concept in Jewish tradition called הידור מצוה/Hiddur Mitzvah, making Mitzvahs beautiful. In the last 20 years we have seen an enormous outpouring of gorgeous Tallitot produced by talented weavers and designers. Dazzling Tallitot are everywhere.

And yet, no matter how beautiful the Beged is, the Tzitzit remain the essence of the Tallit. And the "secret" is in the way the fringes are tied. In brief, part of the symbolism includes: (a) the numerical value of the Hebrew letters of the word ציצית/Tzitzit is 600, there are 5 knots, and 8 strands — totaling 613, the number of Mitzvahs; (b) the specific way the Tzitzit are tied equals the numerical value of one of God's names, and (c) just like tying a string around a finger to remind us of something, the Mitzvah of Tzitzit is to *look* at them and remember all of God's Mitzvahs. For those who, like Rabbi Zuckerman's families, have a thread of blue, the Talmud tells us (Sotah 17a) that the blue resembles the color of the sea, that blue resembles the blue of the sky, the sky like God's Throne of Glory, as Exodus 24:10 describes that under the Throne is a pavement resembling the color of sapphire[12]. Rabbi Zuckerman has brought this message home in a most unique and powerful way, one definitely worth replicating in many other congregations.

The Gifts —
From The Glorious Kid and
For The Glorious Kid

(By Sharon Halper, With Additions By the Author)

From The Bar/Bat Mitzvah Glorious Kid

Did you ever buy a fuchsia-and-orange tie for someone who only wears gray and navy? It's not because you don't like the person. You probably really love him. But you bought it and gave it because fuchsia-and-orange are *your* favorite colors.

We do that all the time. We buy presents that we like for people we love…even if we have really just bought the present *we* would love to receive!

Ideally, gifts are selected with the recipient in mind and combine the sensitivity of the donor with the life of the recipient. Could you perhaps imagine that your Uncle Stanley, the world-renowned software configuration management expert, would not just *love* to decorate his generously-proportioned body with a T-shirt with your face – double life-size — on it? Or that the family accountant would not enjoy a tote bag that says "I survived Chaim Yankel Fefferkorn's Bar Mitzvah luau!"? Or perhaps your friends already have enough photographs of themselves dressed up like a circus star or baseball hero or their favorite jungle animal?

If you can imagine any (or all) of the above, you are ready to think about honoring your guests and the memories of your Bat/Bar Mitzvah with Mitzvah gifts — the sort of gift that keeps the recipient in mind and says all kinds of (wonderful) things about the giver. For many of these suggestions, the Ziv Tzedakah Fund website, www.ziv.org, will be a very useful resource. Interspersed in the suggestions below are a few for programs in Israel. Many more are described on the website, so whatever your idea might be, check ziv.org to see if there is a Mitzvah project in Israel that speaks to your own soul.

The following are just a few match-up possibilities to consider:

For Your Friends: The Rabbanit Bracha Kapach in Jerusalem has provided a wonderful camp for kids for 40 years. She is always in need of funding to pay scholarships and to buy equipment and supplies. Most of the children are from families that struggle to make ends meet, so this would be a *big* Mitzvah. www.ziv.org describes her many other Mitzvah projects in additional to Camp Rabbanit Kapach. Contact Ziv's Agent in Israel, Arnie Draiman for details: soosim@netmedia.net.il.

Find a local family shelter or residential school. Your teacher, rabbi, parents and phone directory can help. Call and ask how many children usually live at the school or shelter and how old the children are. You can be sure that there are never enough baseballs, softballs, hardballs, nerf balls, dodge balls, soccer balls, punch balls, blow-up balls, just plain rubber balls, and Frisbees around the place. After all, have *you* ever had enough of the aforementioned? Others should have the same pleasure.

Buy many – at least one in the name of each friend. Create a pyramid of balls using a box or basket as the base. Wrap the whole wonderful collection in cellophane and decorate with stickers, ribbons, even balloons. You might give your friends an opportunity to add a note or be on the delivery team when the balls go to their new home. Create a certificate for each of your friends, telling them how you honored them. Voilà! Centerpiece, Mitzvah-gift, and lots of smiles from some very happy kids.

Better yet, consider taking a bunch of the kids to a baseball game. Since tickets to professional sports events have become so expensive, consider going to a minor league game. There are three stadiums within an hour drive of my home, and you and the kids will probably have as much fun as if you were at Fenway Park or Camden Yards.

You can do the same kind of Mitzvah buying spree and centerpiece arrangement with books, bubbles, hair-beautifying gizmos, etc. Look around your own room and find something that a large group of children need more of and would love to have.

For the Adults: Adults come in many varieties. Here are some adult sub-groupings:

For Your Teachers, Rabbi, Cantor, and Tutor: Donating money for scholarships for Jewish camps, retreats, and conventions (for adults as well as for kids) would be a wonderful way to honor these people who have worked with you to become educated in All Things Jewish. Books, videos, CDs, DVDs on Jewish topics are also a natural choice. While it might be lovely to give them all air tickets to Israel, these other items are probably more within your budget. Go to your local Jewish bookstore and/or search the web until you see an item that makes you go "Aha! – just perfect for...." Make sure to write a personal inscription in each one, wishing a Yasher Koach for helping you celebrate this great Simcha.

For Elder Relatives and Guests: Donate a Shabbat or holiday dinner for a lonely Elder in honor of each Elder guest. The Elders might be at a local activities center or synagogue. Shabbat dinners and second Seders at synagogues are wonderful for people who don't enjoy family nearby. These meals are often catered and beyond the financial reach of many Elders. Ask your rabbi if *you* can make it possible for someone to attend. Explain that you want to do it anonymously. If you want, you can even take this one step further: Arrange for a food basket to be left at someone's door late at night or early in the morning. If you want to leave a note, write something simple like, "From a friend."

Contact Project Ezra on the Lower East Side of New York for the cost of

home delivery of a holiday food package. Subsidize as many packages as your Tzedakah budget can cover.
[Misha Avramoff, codirector.projectezra@verizon.net, 212-982-3700, www.projectezra.org.]

Bet Frankforter is a wonderful activities center for Elders in Jerusalem. They have a special program where the Elders prepare sandwiches to be delivered to schools for mid-morning snack for students whose families cannot afford it. You could also donate for activities, speakers, field trips, equipment and materials that they need. [frankfor@netvision.net.il]

Call a local activities center for Elders, rehab center, or assisted living facility with limited resources and find out what items they could use. Think of decks of cards in honor of your Poker-playing grandfather or grandmother, a Mah Jongg set in honor of all of your great-aunts, video and audio tapes of Yiddish movies and music, etc. Write a short personal note telling each guest what you've done. They won't even remember if your thank-you notes are short, late, or sloppy. They *will* remember you honored them with an act of Tzedakah.

For People in Healthcare Professions, Or Who Aren't, But Still Care About Their Health: Donate to Dental Volunteers for Israel (DVI), a free children's dental clinic in Jerusalem, founded by an incredible Mitzvah hero, the late Trudi Birger, ז״ל. In your note to the honorees, ask them to spread the word to their dentists that DVI always needs volunteers to work in the clinic. A nice touch would be to include DVI pamphlets with your note to the honorees. [Contact Zev Birger, zevb@netvision.net.il.]

Make a donation to Stop Hunger Now to support its program of inoculations of children in third-world countries. Ray Buchanan, the founder and director, supplies not only food around the world for hungry people, but also critically-needed medicine and medical supplies where there is a desperate need. Include a Stop Hunger Now brochure in the envelope with your note to the honorees. [www.stophungernow.org.]

For Your Parents' Friends and Neighbors: Groups that work with families in transition from shelters to their own homes often provide the simple (but sooo necessary) goods that make independent living possible. You can set up a kitchen with a supply of pots, potholders, utensils, sink items, cleaning supplies, etc. If you are especially creative, try to find an item that begins with the same letter as the honorees' names: frying pan for the Friedmans, pots and pans for the Pietrokovskis, knives for the Knudsens or the Knudelmans (the 'k' is silent).

In Honor of Friends and Relatives With Special Needs: A donation to the Israel National Therapeutic Riding Association (INTRA), which provides therapeutic horseback riding for individuals with a broad range of physical, emotional, and mental disabilities, can provide incredible Life changes for many individuals. Anita Shkedi, the founder, is the actual founder of all therapeutic riding in Israel. Wherever there is a certified center, you will find her students. You can pay for scholarships, buy tack (equipment), and even a horse, which will provide years of benefit for literally hundreds of riders. [intra@012.net.il]

Buy From Israel: Whenever possible, if you are giving something tangible, try to purchase it from an Israeli merchant. It reinforces the importance of Israel for all of the family, and gives critical support to the economy. Just imagine: You buy 123 Havdalah candles of every color and design, you attach a note to each one saying something like, "I love Shabbat. Shabbat lets me think about what is *really* important in life, and Havdallah reminds me to take with me some feeling of Shabbat for the rest of the week. I love light. Light has so many meanings of hope, warmth, caring. I love Israel. I bought these from Yael Levy's Nesher Gift Shop at 27 Ben Yehuda St., Jerusalem, phone 02-398-2223 (n.b.: fictitious name, address and phone number). Because I am so happy you came to share in the Simcha of my Bar/Bat Mitzvah, I am giving you a present with three of the great Loves of My Life — Shabbat, Havdallah, and light — all-in-one." Then you have the pleasure at the party of walking around to each guest and giving out the candles as a very precious thank-you.

Some families give out "favors" to the Bat/Bar Mitzvah's friends, or to the entire list of guests. Giving out tapes and CDs of Israeli music or other items from or about Israel would be an ideal "favor" — though you are not *doing* a favor. You are favoring others with your vision of a world where Israel thrives and its citizens are free to live in peace.

At this point, you may decide to tell your child from which countries you will not buy anything — favors, gifts, food, and decorations, for example — because of their anti-Israel position. This sends an equally-important message to everyone who hears about your "selective buying" policy. After all, many food stores now sell products like "fair trade coffee." This means that the workers in the fields, at the very bottom of the pay and profit scale, receive a better percentage of the store price. And some merchants sell carpets and other items with labels indicating that they were not made by child labor. To buy coffee and carpets selectively because of ethical considerations is commendable. When buying things for Bar/Bat Mitzvah taking an ethical stand about Israel certainly is no less important.

For The Bar/Bat Mitzvah Glorious Kid

Three Introductory Comments:

1. If you are purchasing Jewish books, videos, DVDs, or CDs, for the Bat/Bar Mitzvah, it is perfectly all right if the items will sit on a shelf for a year or two or ten. Years down the road, this same person, perhaps in college or in a new job or involved in a heavy personal relationship, will pull them off the shelf because *the time is right*. This has happened too many times to even begin to count. The same is true for ritual objects like Kiddush cups, Tzedakah boxes, candlesticks, Havdalah sets, and Challah covers. The principle is called, "You Never Know. You Just Never Know," and in the long run, these gifts are a wise investment. In fact, I personally believe they might be a

more important investment than all the stocks and bonds that are put away to provide security for the future. This is a *different kind* of security, one that will not only benefit the individual, but also the Jewish and general community.

2. Even if you give a gift, you may, *in addition,* donate to Tzedakah in the Bat/Bar Mitzvah's honor. One certainly does not preclude the other.

3. Many of the suggestions listed above as presents *from* the Bar/Bat Mitzvah apply for this section for the Bar/Bat Mitzvah.

Educational Materials: *The Encyclopaedia Judaica* is perhaps the most important set of Jewish books available in the English language. Filled with the best research and scholarship, and — well, for lack of a better term — truly encyclopedic in scope, it is 16 volumes in print. The wonderful news is that the "EJ" is now out on CD-ROM for $129.00. Friends and relatives can join together to get this for the Bat/Bar Mitzvah.

Heritage: Civilization and The Jews is a dazzling DVD set with video clips, maps, narratives, incredible cross references and an awesome wealth of information. Any young person can surf and do research with ease — all for less than $100.

Other books, CD-ROMs and similar materials might include: a good Hebrew-English Biblical text (Jewish Publication Society's *Tanakh* is superb), a good Hebrew-English/English Hebrew dictionary, books about Israel, including "coffee table books" with many pictures, "coffee table" books on other Jewish topics, books on Jewish values (Rabbi Joseph Telushkin's books are particularly fine volumes), books of Jewish quotes, DVDs of important Jewish movies such as "Schindler's List," CDs of Jewish music, to name just a few.

You may buy the books yourself, or give a gift certificate to a Jewish bookstore or website.

Ritual Objects: *Tallit, Tallit* bag, a special *kippah* — most parents purchase these for their child as part of the overall necessities of the event. However, many other items such as a lovely Tzedakah box, Shabbat candlesticks, Menorah, and Havdalah set are left for "later on" in the hazy future when the young person has grown up enough to realize she or he should own one. You may wish to "get the jump" on things and get them *now* so your daughter or son won't miss out on many good years of using *their very own* Jewish ritual items.

All Kinds of Miscellaneous "Things," Tchatchkas, Fun Items From Israel: Israeli music CDs, t-shirts, maps, posters, prints, artwork, wall hangings to fill her or his bedroom with Jewish images and presence, jewelry, cosmetics, skin care products, again, just to name a few.

Throw a Party for Israeli Soldiers: Relatives and friends may wish to honor the Bat/Bar Mitzvah by making a pizza or schwarma party for Israeli soldiers. (You can even arrange to take a group of soldiers to lunch or dinner, as Benjamin Salman of Carmichael, CA did.) On several occasions, Ziv Tzedakah Fund has been involved when the Bat/Bar Mitzvah

Soldiers serving near Tiberias were treated to a delicious dinner made possible by Benjamin Salman of Carmichael, California, who donated some of his Bar Mitzvah Tzedakah money to pay for the event.

has paid for the party, but, there is no objection to others doing it, too. In fact, there is no real need to wait for a Big Simcha as B'nai/B'not Mitzvah to have one of these parties. You might want to celebrate יום העצמעות/Yom HaAtzma'ut, Israel Independence Day, but that, too is a major event, and rather obvious. For a birthday — even one that is not a multiple of 10 — is also good. Waking up one day and feeling particularly good, that's a good reason to celebrate. Pick any time, even that moment when you finally figured out how to download digital photos on your computer — share the good feelings. It will make many soldiers very happy.

One Final Note: Some families have established a fine Hanukkah custom. *If* they give gifts, they ask the children to pick one night when the gift they receive will be given, in turn, to someone else who may not be fortunate enough to have the money to own it. I have heard of parents who do the same with the Bar/Bat Mitzvah gifts. They ask their daughter or son to pick one of the gifts and to decide where to give it away. This is just one more way to share the Simcha, the joy of this great moment in the life of their child.

The Mitzvah Project/
Mitzvah Money

Why Do Mitzvahs...
And Not Just Now?

הִנֵּה תָּאַבְתִּי לְפִקֻּדֶיךָ בְּצִדְקָתְךָ חַיֵּנִי׃

I love your Mitzvahs.
Give me Life through Your Tzedakah. *(Psalm 119:40)*

*I*n the classic Jewish context, one should do Mitzvahs because they are just that — Mitzvahs. They are God's commandments, guides on how this awesome gift called "Life" may be appreciated and put to holy use. As mentioned in other sections of the book, one of the first instructions God gives to Abraham is:

כִּי יְדַעְתִּיו לְמַעַן אֲשֶׁר יְצַוֶּה אֶת־בָּנָיו וְאֶת־בֵּיתוֹ אַחֲרָיו
וְשָׁמְרוּ דֶּרֶךְ יְהוָה לַעֲשׂוֹת צְדָקָה וּמִשְׁפָּט

For I have selected him [Abraham]
so that he may instruct his children and his posterity after him
to keep God's ways:
to do what is just and right. [Tzedakah U'Mishpat] (Genesis 18:19)

Mitzvahs are Mitzvahs, and Jews are supposed to do Mitzvahs. Personally, I find this very appealing. However, I (again, personally) am at ease with many other *reasons* why people may want to do Mitzvahs. Before you read my list, it might be worthwhile making one of your own.

Some of the reasons on my own list: People like the sense of accomplishment; they feel in their heart, mind, and soul, *and in their bones* that while they see everywhere how power can be abusive and is abused, power can be a great human blessing; that they are not helpless in the face of seemingly-insurmountable woe and trouble in the world; that they *can* change lives for the better; they feel good about what they are doing, and feel good about themselves. This last reason is particularly appealing to me.

Educators, social workers, and every kind of therapist are concerned about and encounters individuals who have lost their self-image. Many fine methods of dealing with human dignity and self-image have been developed over the years. Therapists and social workers are involved with building and re-building self-image every day. Classroom teachers, educational researchers, camp counselors, sports coaches, and those who teach ropes courses are also involved. Each one, in turn, uses his or her own skills to allow the patients, students, players, wards, and campers to develop fully as human beings with a strong feeling of self worth. I would personally add to the list all individuals who teach, train, and encourage people to become Mitzvah People. Mitzvah people, and Mitzvahs heroes, do no less for the people with whom they work. In many ways, because of the broad range and reach of Mitzvahs, the self-image-building results may be even more impressive.

In the final Jewish analysis, Mitzvahs are still Mitzvahs and essentially why I, personally, believe people should do Mitzvahs. In the *final* final analysis, all of the other motivations mentioned above yield great benefits, and that really is what is most important.

One other note about the benefits of Mitzvahs. One of our Jewish texts (Leviticus Rabba 34:8) teaches us:

תני בש' ר' יהושע

יותר ממה שבעל הבית עושה עם העני

העני עושה עם בעל הבית

It was taught in the name of Rabbi Yehoshua,
"The poor person [standing at the door]
does more for the house-holder
than the householder does for the poor person."

It may be that the great Rabbi Yehoshua was exaggerating a little to make his point. First and foremost are the benefits to the recipient — food, shelter, dignity, care, cure, hope. Mitzvahs in the purest sense are to be done without any expectation of reward, recognition, or thanks. Still, Rabbi Yehoshua teaches, that built in to the very act of Tzedakah are a long list of Good Things for those who choose to do Tikkun Olam, you feel good because you did something good, you have an image of yourself that's healthy and strong, an image that you are made in the image of God.

What Doing Mitzvahs Feels Like

The following is a long string of non-sequential images about what it might feel like when you are just about to do a Mitzvah, are doing it, have finished it, a second afterwards — a little like physicists calculating What It Was All Like one millionth of a milli-second after The Big Bang — what having done a Mitzvah or many Mitzvahs feels like a week, a month, a year, or years later. Choose which one feels right to you. Make your own list. (Composed with a little help from my friends.)

It feels

like, all of a sudden, you could pick up a brush, stand in front of a blank canvas, and paint a masterpiece, like Rembrandt;

like sitting in front of 88 white and black keys, never having played the piano, and, all of a sudden, the people jamming the concert hall are on their feet whistling, clapping, stomping their feet, and shouting, "Encore, Encore!"

like the ski jumper seconds off the ramp, soaring in silence, high above the crowd;

like the hawk on high, and its sister, the eagle, circling on the warm heavenly drafts of air, at ease and at home;

like the rush of the jet beginning its roll down the runway, the pilot having just pushed the levers all the way forward, and, at the same time, in the process and act — at the beginning, middle, and end of a Mitzvah — like a safe landing, touch down, sometimes after the thunderstorm raged all around at 30,000 feet, lightning flashing like at Sinai overhead;

like a vast garden, — though you may not know the names of each flower beyond carnations and roses — flowers delighting the eye, fragrances too sweet for mere words, even poetry, the family works together, cuts here, arranges there, and presents a bouquet never to be forgotten, though the petals fade with time, to an Elder all alone Lo, these many years;

like you are the miner who found the diamond in the rough, then cut it ever-so-delicately and polished it, fashioned the perfect setting (jewelers all agree), with your own hands and ingenuity, and set the jewel in the ring for the couple so very much in love or maybe for The Queen's crown for a royal occasion, i.e., life;

like the doctor saying, "You're cured beyond remission, cured, I say.

There are no traces, none, there is not one single malevolent cell left in your body";

like the minute after the flu is gone;

like the day winter left which you only paid attention to until sometime later on, having been surprised by crocuses or daffodils all of a sudden right there in full color;

like when shoes no longer pinch or squeeze your foot;

like when you were little and that one aunt would pinch your cheek — and it hurt — but you grew older and you forgave her...she had her reasons;

like when you were a little kid you had a friend who used to pinch your cheek when he would see you but it hurt, it always hurt, and you wondered why he did it? always, I say always, against what, against whom was he lashing out and taking it out on you? but always and above it all it hurt until one day you stand up for yourself and depending on your mood say, "Don't!" or "Please don't" or "Just don't do it any more" is what it's like when life hurts and people hurt until you say you won't let it happen any more. Mitzvahs stop the hurting;

like Mommy or Daddy kissing away the scrape, the cut, the hurt and the tears;

like pulling away the hand that's running the fingernails across the blackboard;

like when clothes that could fit anyone stop being new and fit your body only;

like the moment when you finished your first full sentence in Hebrew ever and you clap for joy and say to your friend, "חברה, מה אתם חושבים?" - Well, how about that? I did it all by myself!";

like the missing spice for the soup, taking from the bottles on the rack and sprinkling, tasting, and proclaiming to the kitchen assembly, "Ah, delicious," even if you took — not paying attention as much as you should have — the wrong one by mistake, and it became the right one anyhow, delicious;

like your computer crashed and everything is lost, data, pictures, shows, the works and you try this and that to trick it back to life until you give in and call in a geek who says, "Please step into the other room and leave me alone" and an hour later they say, it's all right, it's all fixed, everything is OK;

like cats of every size and pelt and length of whiskers drowsing in the sun;

like the leap into the pool, — too cold by three degrees — into the groove of strokes, you, modest in expectation, how far you go on that day not so important, the pleasantness of body-and-soul as you dry yourself;

like tasting your favorite piece of cake oozing with chocolate and chunks of chocolate chips and chocolate icing after not having done so in a while, either a short or long while makes no difference;

like the perfect cookie, the one you baked yourself, with your mother and son together....for the basket right before dawn left at the door for someone hard-pressed for a treat, money run out because and because, for too many "becauses," and now taste of life renewed;

like the memory of school when you first drew outside of the thick printed lines in the book, used the color not recommended by the teacher, and, well, it looked just fine to you, so you knew it was all right though try as you might 40 years later to figure out why you did it you can't — Was I not good enough? Did I just not want to do what the teacher said I should do?;

like watching your Eema or Abba take away the training wheels from your bike as you stand there balancing it, your heart eager, ready to ride all on your own, fast, slow, as you please, all by yourself, you as a child, as your heart so moves you, free;

like driving on your own in your first brand-new car for the first time, even though your first car might not have been brand-new, your first brand-new one is different, a whole new feeling;

like your first pair of glasses slipped over your ears by the optometrist for the final fit, bending, adjusting ever so slightly, she says, "Now turn around and look out the window" and you are so in disbelief of what your eyes behold, words fail you and you sigh for the past because you couldn't, didn't see it all so you stand and press your face against the glass to see it all better, the world, people one by one, in pairs and groups, masses, motion and color, life as you hadn't seen it in years but remember once — perhaps as a child at play — how it was and how it is supposed to be, and how, now that you can see, how, indeed, it can be;

like opening that present you've always wanted on your birthday, even though you are old enough to say to friends "Presents aren't really that important" but you still know now and again they're nice to have;

like finding the perfect quote;

like finding a friend for Life;

like the moment you watch your baby being born, which is so self-understood you don't need to say anything else or explain to anyone because it is so clear, so in a class by itself in the entire picture of Life;

like coming home;

like finding yourself which is really finding yourself-through-others;

like the house so very very clean for Passover;

like on a night so bone-chilling cold and your comforter so big you climb into bed, settle in and say crazy as it seems, "There must be a blessing for comforters";

like love at first sight;

like love after forty years;

like the first time your eyes opened really wide when you realized they were lying to you when they said things like, "Winning isn't the most important thing...it's the only thing" and "There's just nothing more we or anyone can do about it";

like loving The Little Train That Could and then you are 28 and someone reminds you of it and you say, "It just isn't so," and you feel tricked that such a bad message was given to you when you were so young and you are sad life isn't like that, but sometime later on you come to know that if that train can't make it up the hill all by itself, then someone, somewhere will give it a hand, that everything can be fixed;

like loving The Giving Tree until someone says, "But at the end there's nothing left of the tree at all except a stump," and you say, "It was a good story up until right before the end, but Silverstein blew it," and you wished you had had a chance while he was still alive to say to him, "Ah, Shel, with all due respect, you should have thought instead about that starfish story. You would have understood this, gotten it, and held it dear as a great truth, that the one who was throwing the beached starfish back into the ocean one by one — child, man, woman, old man or woman, however you picture the story — she or he didn't get tired from it, didn't wear out, but, to the contrary, got stronger and stronger with each starfish's life she or he saved," and you start to ask around for an eloquent, lyrical re-write author in English like Keats (God rest his soul) or that woman — Marguerite Henry (a search engine helped me find the name in a split second, God rest her soul) who came to my school in the third grade who wrote about the horses living wild on an island off the Maryland coast, Misty of Chincoteague, that had, as I recall, a very happy ending to it, I would have told Shel to start all over again, maybe instead with a sequoia or something really big that they tell me doesn't die, it just lives and lives and lives until something outside of it does it in, but wouldn't have died on its own, not on your life;

like the dawn, the only dawn of its kind anywhere on earth, over Jerusalem on Shabbat as the early risers stroll to Minyan to hear the words of the Almighty who made Heaven and Earth by word which was, in truth, a deed, an act of lovingkindess for us to imitate;

like dusk and sunset, the only dusk and sunset of its kind in the world, settling over Jerusalem at the end of Shabbat, minutes, only minutes away from wine, spice, and candle flames, your soul at peace.

3 Things to Remember
When Doing Mitzvahs

1. **Mitzvahs give us the power of life and death.**
   We can save lives. *Anyone* can. Through Mitzvahs.
   I have asked thousands of teen-agers, "How many of you have a parent who is in a life-saving profession?" Almost every single hand raised was from a child of a doctor.

   Incomplete answer. Wrong answer.

   All of us are in a life-saving profession. Just consider the well-known and truly awesome teaching from the Talmud (Mishna Sanhedrin, Chapter 4, end):

   וכל המקיים נפש אחת מעלה עליו הכתוב כאלו קים עולם מלא

   ....Whoever saves a single life —
   it is as if that person had saved an entire world.

   For nearly 30 years a considerable portion of my Mitzvah work has been devoted to preventing people from dying or suffering for all the wrong reasons. To put it more bluntly, many people are in pain and without hope for all the wrong reasons. Just a few of those reasons are in anguish and danger include loneliness, helplessness, boredom, powerlessness, uselessness, chronic human unhappiness, fatigue of the spirit and weariness of the soul; loss of the will-to-live, a sense of abandonment, wariness of those who mean well but perform poorly or maliciously — all their energies being exhausted fighting off *the good intentions* of those who harm them in the name of their personal health and welfare, and not being listened to when they say what is in their hearts because they wouldn't look into their eyes while they were pouring out their hearts.

   This so-called fact-of-life — "People die. What can I do about it?" — can be reversed significantly through Mitzvahs, as our tradition teaches us (Midrash on Psalms 41:3):

   אמר ר' יונה...שמסתכל וחושב עליו היאך להחיותו

   Rabbi Yonah said,
   ....The person-doing-Tzedakah should take an intense look
   at the Mitzvah situation at hand
   and consider the best way
   to give the other person back his or her decent and dignified Life.

2. **Judaism asks us to use all our talents and human resources — *all* of them — to solve difficult, even terrible, human situations.** Our brains, our ability to sew, to dance, to hug, to dream, to use our imaginations, energy, wisdom and insight in any combination which best suits our own spiritual, physical, and psychological make-up. When we are fixing the world, every ability *can* be and *should* be put in the service of Mitzvahs, as our tradition teaches us (Jerusalem Talmud, Pe'ah 8:8):

א'ד יונה...הדא דמסתכל במצוה היאך לעשותה

Rabbi Yonah said,
....The person-doing-Tzedakah
should examine the Tzedakah-situation thoroughly
in order to find the best way possible to perform the Mitzvah.

3. **Mitzvahs are a privilege...**not a burden, not something to get credit for, not something to grumble about while doing them. A *privilege,* and surely one of Life's great blessings. Once again, our tradition addresses this all-important subject (Leviticus Rabba 34:1 [Margoliot 4:773]):

א"ר יונה...הוי מסתכל בו היאך לזכות בו

Rabbi Yonah said,
....The person-doing-Tzedakah
should examine the Tzedakah-situation thoroughly
and keep in mind how *it is a privilege to do the Mitzvah* through that person.

Choosing Your Mitzvah Project

אמר רבי אלעזר...שצדיקים אומרים מעט ועושים הרבה

Rabbi Elazar Says:
Tzaddikim-Good People say little and do much. (*Bava Metzia 87a*)

Useful Tools, Ideas, and Jewish Texts to Help You Choose

The number of possible ways to Fix the World are nearly infinite. You will want to pick one that is a combination of what *feels right and comfortable* for you, what really *needs* to be done, and what *you actually think you can do*. Keep in mind that there is no such thing as a small Mitzvah. Everything you do, every so-called little thing, is not little. *Everything* you do makes a difference and changes the world and people's lives.

Over the past 29 years, I have found that most B'nai and B'not Mitzvah I have learned about accomplish much more than he or she ever thought possible.

The website of my Tzedakah project, Ziv Tzedakah Fund, **www.ziv.org,** is an excellent starting point. In the 2004 Annual Report, there are more than 100 Mitzvah heroes and projects listed, almost all of them with web links describing their incredibly fine Tikkun Olam work. You may also find it useful to download "So You Are Becoming a Bar/Bat Mitzvah," "116 Practical Mitzvah Suggestions," "Opportunities for Direct Assistance in Israel," and other featured selections. "www.ziv.org, The Web, Google, and Mitzvahs" in this book will also provide you with more detailed and practical information. All of them should make it easier in your search for just the right Mitzvah project *for you*.

The 6 Most Useful Jewish Questions To Ask

When it comes to choosing a Mitzvah project, the following questions will help you focus on which one is best for you:

1. What am I good at? (Sometimes asked as, "What am I *really* good at?")

2. What do I like to do? (Sometimes asked as, "What do I *really* like to do?)

3. What bothers me so much about what is wrong in the world that I get

really angry and want to do something about it?

4. What can I do *right now,* today, in the next week, or in the period leading up to my Bar/Bat Mitzvah to make a difference?

5. Whom do I know?

6. Why not?

Over the past few years, I have noticed that #3 often provides the best, most deeply-felt response, *and* the best Mitzvah project. It would be beneficial if you and your parents spent some time making a list of those things that are happening in the world that are so bad or wrong or troubling, and then work from there as to what *exactly* can be done to change it.

You may want to work variations on these questions, or to create entirely new questions — whatever will fit your own and your family's specific abilities. Some have suggested, "What are you (really) bad at, but might try if you knew it was a way to make a certain Mitzvah happen?" and "What *don't* you really like to do or hate to do, but might try if you knew it was a way to make a certain Mitzvah happen?" None of the questions are holy or engraved in stone. They are simply meant to help you find the best Mitzvah project for yourself as a unique individual about to embark on a life of Mitzvahs.

After doing this exercise, and after the Mitzvah project is selected and is completed, you may have discovered one particular Mitzvah that is "dear to your heart," My teacher and friend, Yosef Ben Shlomo Hacohen, has coined a fine term for this — your **"Mitzvah Major."** Following his lead, we would say that the process of selecting the right Mitzvah for your Mitzvah Major is similar to the steps you will go through when you select your field of study in college. I would add: Choosing your Mitzvah Major is at least of equal importance to picking your college major. Yosef continues by reminding us that, "Just like having a major in college does not mean that one should neglect other areas of knowledge, so too, having a 'Mitzvah Major' does not mean that we should neglect other good and holy deeds. The purpose of choosing a Mitzvah Major is to develop the unique talents and strengths within each of us so that we can make a greater contribution to Tikkun Olam."

In the final analysis, there may be one more added long-term benefit. Looking back, parents and child will be able to remember this process — choosing a Mitzvah project, and perhaps discovering a Mitzvah Major — as a shared experience whose significance will be seen and felt in almost every aspect of your shared — and individual — lives. You and your parents will have that much more in common to talk about.

A Note to Parents: On occasion, I have been told stories about pre-B'not/B'nai Mitzvah who have not been terribly enthusiastic about doing a Mitzvah project. Mothers and fathers have used terms ranging from "indifferent" to "apathetic" to "profoundly reticent," even "withdrawn." While there are no miracle techniques to encourage your child to open up, be assured that underneath the surface is a caring heart, willing to do good for others. A parent, sometimes with the help of friends, teachers, the rabbi or cantor, just needs to find some opening into that cardiac-spiritual chamber. If these 6 questions don't work, keep trying. My years of experience tell me that *some* technique exists that will help bring out the best in your child.

The Most Useful Jewish Text I Have Ever Found

Using your talents, time, and Tzedakah money to do Tikkun Olam means that you want to do something good for someone else. On the surface, that seems simple enough, but since there are countless ways to Fix the World, how do you focus on something very specific to do? Above all else, remember to concentrate on the *other person's* needs. Jewish tradition helps you in that search. In his ספר המצוות/Sefer HaMitzvot, Maimonides counts, one by one, all 613 Mitzvot in the Torah. In Positive Mitzvah 206, he gives an extremely brief and articulate definition of exactly what the Torah means when it says that we are commanded to love others as we love ourselves. (Leviticus 19:18). The verse is not as easy to understand as one would think at first glance. Does it mean to love others in the same way we love ourselves, as much as we love ourselves, *at least as much* as we love ourselves? Maimonides gives us some very valuable insight:

וכל מה-שארצה לעצמי ארצה לו כמוהו
וכל-מה-שלא ארצה לעצמי ולידידי
לא ארצה לו בשבילו כמוהו

Whatever I want for myself,
I want the same for that other person.
And whatever I do not want for myself or my friends,
I do not want for that other person.

After you have read the text a few times and discussed it, you may find it useful to make two separate and *very personal* lists: (1) what you *do* want for yourself, and what you *do not* want for yourself. Both the positive and the negative are important. Sometimes a positive has four or five negative opposites and vice versa. For example, the opposite of "good health" can be disease, disability, physical illness, mental illness, anxiety, or just "feeling bad." The opposite of "to be loved" can cover the range from to be hated, to be unloved, to be disliked, or to be ignored. It is also important to be very specific. To list "to have enough money not only to survive but also to enjoy life" is better than to just write "to make a living" (someday when you are older). The former positive statement then offers you many negatives: to be poor, to always worry about being poor, to barely scrape by, to have enough for food, clothing and shelter, but not enough to take my family out for a nice day at the beach, to be homeless — all of which can give you ideas for your Mitzvah project.

Helpful Strategies

First, and of greatest importance, the Glorious Bar/Bat Mitzvah Kid should think of and **list absolutely every Mitzvah project** he or she might want to do. This should include *anything and everything that comes to mind.* Parents should do the same, making a list of absolutely every Mitzvah project they think their child might want to do... *anything and everything that comes to mind.* If you try to think "Mitzvahs" as much as possible, you may come up with an idea from something someone said just as an off-hand comment, you saw in one of your books or in a movie, or even something you heard in a song. Some of the best Mitzvah projects have come from the most unexpected places. Always keep in mind that even if you think a specific project is impractical or too big for one person or family to manage, still, add it to the list. All too often, a Mitzvah project never comes to fruition because in this early stage, it is eliminated as un-doable.

Give yourselves time. Let the ideas work their way around your mind and imagination. In fact, it would be good to leave the lists in a drawer for a week or two. You will need time to pause and let the project-ideas roll around in the back of your mind and the intricate circuitry of your imagination.

While yours and your parents' lists may overlap in certain areas, there will be differences, and the combined lists may ultimately produce the ideal Mitzvah project. Even from the earliest days of Bat/Bar Mitzvah Mitzvah projects, some of the best projects came from (a) The Glorious Kid, (b) a parent, (c) both parents, (d) a combination of (a), (b), and (c). Do keep in mind that the greatest long-term effect on The Glorious Kid is provided by a project you, yourself, either thought of, designed, or made very real.

Also, during this preliminary period, talk about your lists with your rabbi, cantor, teachers, friends, and relatives. They may come up with additional ideas that are built on your own, help you refine your raw material, or assist and direct you in figuring out how your Mitzvah idea can become real-live Tikkun Olam.

Ideally, the project should be tied to that week's Torah reading. For example, for Parshat נֹחַ/Noach: You could easily tie in animal-assisted therapy, such as Avshalom Beni's marvelous work in Israel. [www.ziv.org/ar2004/ar2004.pdf] Or for any of the first five Torah readings in the Book of Exodus, how your donation to The North American Conference on Ethiopian Jewry (NACOEJ) helps bring Ethiopian Jews to freedom in Israel. [www.nacoej.org] Your rabbi and teachers should be able to help you with this aspect of your Bat/Bar Mitzvah.

Once you have done all of this, you are ready for The Second Round: Using some of the resources mentioned above, narrow down the list, start surfing the web, and check out any other resources you might think will help. Ask questions such as, "Can I relate this to Israel?", "Will others respond to the project itself and my personal enthusiasm?", "Can this be accomplished by the time of my Bar/Bat Mitzvah?", and "What happens to all the good I have brought into the world the day, the week, the month, the year, many years *after* my Bar/Bat Mitzvah?"

Finally, don't be discouraged or put off by the last question. You are ready now to **just do it,** to change people's lives and the world. In the end, only good comes of it.

Whenever I talk about Mitzvah projects, I think of Elana Erdstein, who collected 25,000 bars of soap, shampoos, hair conditioners, and hand cream tubes that people had collected from hotels. She donated these Mitzvah items to shelters for victims of domestic violence and for homeless people. It was really quite an awesome accomplishment. But, thinking about it over the years, I realized that the very first one she donated had all the power needed to change a life. Because of the chance to wash out his or her hair with a classy shampoo, a person feeling wretched and heartbroken might once again feel like a human being with dignity. To put it in visual terms, think of Star Wars. Picture the green ray of light coming from whatever they called their anti-forces-of-evil weapons. The surge of power was awesome. That's how much power was in each mini-bottle of shampoo, tube of hand cream, every bar of soap, Elana collected and donated. *That's* how much power is in *any* Mitzvah you do for your Bar or Bat Mitzvah.

Beyond "finally," don't rule out the possibility of doing more than one Mitzvah project. Two or more can be related to each other, or they can be totally separate because you want to make an impact on more than one area of Tikkun Olam. So don't be deceived just because people refer to "The Bar/Bat Mitzvah's Bar/Bat Mitzvah Mitzvah Project." It is just as easy to say, "The Bar/Bat Mitzvah's Bar/Bat Mitzvah Mitzvah *Projects.*"

A Very Partial List of Some Projects Others Have Done

One category of Mitzvah projects is **Collections for People In Need:** food, clothing — all types: baby clothing, warm clothing for people who live on the streets, fun clothing for children — and accessories, soaps, shampoos, conditioner and skin cream from hotels that people have collected and are sitting on a shelf in a closet, cosmetics, old cell phones to be donated to victims of domestic violence and other people in need such as school bus drivers, crossing guards, elderly people living alone, and similar vulnerable individuals ("911" still works), stuffed animals, games, books, videos, sports equipment, sports videos, eye glasses, over-the-ear hearing aids, musical instruments, wigs and baseball caps for people losing their hair in cancer treatments. In most collection cases, the process is simple: First locate where the items will be donated, then publicize in any appropriate fashion your Mitzvah collection. In some situations, there are details that you should explain to those who will join you in your act of Tikkun Olam. The following are examples of three such collections, and the necessary information you would need to provide:

Used Cellphones

1. **Why?** Old cellphones still dial "911," and the service is free. Old and de-activated cell phones are donated to victims of domestic violence and other people in need, such as school bus drivers, crossing guards, elderly people living alone, and similar vulnerable individuals.

2. **How?** Contact your local police domestic violence unit or the community's domestic violence network. Most will accept and donate the phones to the appropriate recipients.

   Important: Ask your police domestic violence unit or domestic violence network **how many phones are needed** and proceed accordingly. *Always* collect as many as you can. I cannot stress enough that some groups that do *not* need more phones may be selling them for their salvage value. This is not what you want. So check carefully when you make the arrangements. If they have more than they need, find another group that *will* distribute them on your behalf to people in need.

3. **Do it:** Having done your research, begin the collection at the synagogue, school, or other agency. Do not wait until you have large numbers of phones — take them in as frequently as possible as they come in. Each may be a life-saving Mitzvah cellphone.

Kid Videos

1. **Why?** Kids in the hospital suffer from sickness, pain, fatigue, weariness of body *and* boredom of mind and soul. Videos make a difference, a *big* difference. Hospitals all have VCRs, so videos are always in demand.

2. **How?**
   A. Set up a meeting with a staff member of the pediatric unit in a local hospital. Tell him or her that you are planning to organize a drive to collect gently-used videos.

   B. The Breakthrough: Meryl Innerfield, a young woman celebrating her Bat Mitzvah on Long Island launched such a collection drive, but with the following all-important proviso — *the child in the hospital gets to take the favorite video home.* Her reasoning was simple: When you think about it, why in the world would you make a child-patient return the video? Hasn't it been tough enough just being sick and in the hospital? Why should the child add one more element of unhappiness to the hospital experience by being told "No, you can't take *The Lion King* home with you"?

Meryl Innerfield of Wantagh, NY, with "kid" videos she donated to a local hospital as her Bat Mitzvah Mitzvah project.

   C. This should be explained to the hospital staff. You should launch your drive only if they accept this condition. The obvious problem that they may run out of videos is not the child-patient's problem. It is the problem of the community to keep supplying them

3. **Do It:** Launch the drive in your synagogue, school, among friends. Deliver the videos. There are many thousands of them out there waiting to be donated.

Infant Car Seats

1. Why? There are so many families "out there" that do not have car seats for their infants, putting the child at great risk.

2. How? Find the place that will accept and distribute the car seats. Make phone calls, meet the people in charge of distribution. Start with local social service agencies, Jewish Family Service, and law enforcement departments. People at those agencies will also give you all the information you need about which car seats meet federal standards. Then, when you publicize your project, indicate that you are collecting car seats manufactured after the approved date.

3. Do it: Launch the drive.

Andrew Cohen of Highland Park, NJ, poses as Jinggles, the Mitzvah Clown. Andrew enjoys clowning and made it his Bar Mitzvah Mitzvah Project. He is still visiting local nursing homes and other places where people might need some laughs, good cheer, and pleasant conversation.

Besides collection-type Mitzvah projects, the entire world of Tikkun Olam is open before you. The following (in absolutely no order at all) is **an incredibly short list of other Mitzvah projects** some Glorious Bar and Bat Mitzvah *kinderlach* have done: sponsored pizza and schwarma parties for Israeli soldiers; wrote a cookbook and donated the proceeds of the sales; established a local division of Challenger Baseball for Little League; made dreams come true for residents of a nursing home — the Kid then became not only a Bar Mitzvah, but also a Dreamweaver [The Second Wind Dreams Program: www.secondwind.org]; bought birds, bought an aquarium for a nursing home; became a Mitzvah clown like Andrew Cohen of Highland Park, NJ, www.mitzvahclowns.com]; raised a service dog for training to be given to an individual with special needs; many cut and donated their own hair to make wigs for kids with permanent hair loss due to a disease called alopecia (and for other reasons); decorated and donated caps for adults and kids losing their hair because of cancer treatments; rebuilt and upgraded computers for individuals unable to pay for the upgrades and service; borrowed animals from the local animal shelter and went to visit dying people in hospice; held an old-time bake sale and donated the proceeds to Tzedakah, and so many more creative Mitzvah project ideas, too many to list.

An additional category of Mitzvah projects is **an incredibly short list that includes some that Glorious Bar and Bat Mitzvah *kinderlach* may have already done, but I haven't heard about them yet:** purchased large print prayerbooks for the synagogue; purchased magnifying glasses and made them available for worshippers with visual impairments; were instrumental in getting a special sound system for hearing-impaired people for the synagogue; paid for an interpreter and invited members of the deaf community to come to the Bar/Bat Mitzvah; took friends and did "Mitzvah manicures" at shelters and nursing homes; publicized various little-known Mitzvah projects around their community [see www.ziv.org for various suggestions]; arranged for a deluxe visit to a hairdresser for women in shelters; with friends and family: repaired, cleaned up, and spruced up, a house of someone no longer able to do it for himself or herself; organized a program to provide rides for people who don't drive to come to synagogue, organized a group of friends to fix up a cemetery that had fallen into disrepair...and many, many more.

The Alpert family, members of Valley Beth Shalom in Encino, CA, is blessed with four daughters. Each of them had a Bat Mitzvah that exemplified all that this section "Choosing a Mitzvah Project" describes. They were creative in their research and in the variety of Tikkun Olam they accomplished. For families that want to find out more about Sarra's, Alana's, Aaren's, and Adina's projects and to discuss possible adaptations and additional Mitzvah ideas, contact Merrill Alpert at alpyone@aol.com.

In addition, there are several other **special categories of Mitzvah projects.** For example, **twinning.** There are many opportunities to twin with someone else on your Bar/Bat Mitzvah day. Three possible choices are (1) twinning with an Ethiopian Jewish Child in Israel. [Go to the website of The North American Conference on Ethiopian Jewry, www.nacoej. org], (2) twinning with a non-Jewish person who risked his or her life to save Jews during the שואה/Shoah, Holocaust. [The Jewish Foundation for The Righteous, www.jfr.org], and (3) twinning with a child who did not survive the שואה/Shoah, Holocaust: it will not be difficult for you to find an organization that will supply the Bar/Bat Mitzvah with a biography of such a child, which the Bar/Bat Mitzvah includes in his or her speech to the congregation.

Other Bar/Bat Mitzvah Mitzvah projects included **working with and/or providing for individuals with special needs in the community.** A simple example would be the following: Have your synagogue consolidate all tools, devices, and instruments relating to people with special needs of any kind — including language differences — on a table *outside* the sanctuary door, with a sign in BIG letters. On the table should be (1) large-print *Siddurim*/prayerbooks and *Chumashim*/texts of the Torah and Haftarot, (2) Siddurim and Chumashim, with Russian, Spanish, Farsi translations, or any other language that some congregants will need, (3) a variety of magnifying glasses, and (4) earphones for the special sound system for hearing-impaired individuals. (For congregations that do not activate electrical devices on Shabbat and holidays, there is still a need for these sound-enhancing items for week-day events such as lectures and meetings, and for use on days when electricity is permitted such as week-day minyans, Hanukkah, Purim, Rosh Chodesh, and Chol HaMo'ed.) This Mitzvah project is of extreme importance, because it eliminates the need for the congregant to ask someone. For many people, this is humiliating. More often than not, they will not ask, and, as a result, they will spend their time at your Bar/Bat Mitzvah missing out on so much of the experience. Whichever ones you do, you will be considerably raising the consciousness of the congregation.

There is one additional area of Mitzvah work relating to people with special needs that you may want to explore. There are still a few congregations that do not have the above-listed items because they feel they have no members who will need them. You might want to make an appointment with the rabbi and president to have them reconsider their approach. You would want to advocate for the position that, if the congregation *had* these devices, people with special needs would make it a point of coming. Take a look at the Sunday newspaper religion section. Many of the churches have logos and symbols indicating that they have wheelchair access, hearing devices, sign language interpreting, and similar methods for reaching out to all members of the community.

Finally, one of my very favorite categories I call **(It's OK) — Radical, Far-Out, Offbeat Projects.** I am completely aware, of course, that one person's "far-out" is another's "Well, let's just do it!" Remember that, in The Early Days, when the first few B'nai/B'not Mitzvah did any Mitzvah projects at all, some people made them feel either like goody-goodies or weird. The very idea of Bar/Bat Mitzvah Mitzvah Projects was considered radical, far-out, or offbeat. We owe it to rabbis such as Bernard King, formerly of Shir HaMa'alot in Newport Beach, CA, and a few others, who made it acceptable — without any peer and family pressure *not* to do it.

So here are a few (at least people think at the moment) radical, far-out, or offbeat ideas to make your Grand Event a little more special: If you want to bring in a Mitzvah hero — one of the Giants of Tikkun Olam — or scholar-in-residence to speak and share their Mitzvahs and Torah at your event, then just do it. A few people have already done so, possibly starting a trend for others to do the same. One Wonder Kid built a ramp to the Bima with her father to provide wheelchair access for congregants and visitors. *Dad and daughter with their own hands.* Another magnificent young man — one of Rabbi King's sons — took kids from a shelter for homeless people to a baseball game. One of our Glorious, Magnificent *Kinderlach* sponsored a Songs of Love event, to provide an individual song for a child with a life-threatening illness. [www.songsoflove.org.] One Bat Mitzvah decided she wanted to have the ceremony and reception at the local Jewish nursing home where she had made many friends during the months of her Mitzvah-project visits. One of my favorites: The family made gourmet doggie treats, sold them, then donated the money to the Israel Guide Dog Center for the Blind. [igdcb@nni.com.] And yet another far-out, offbeat radical Bar Mitzvah asked guests to purchase and donate new underwear for shelters. In my opinion, this was a very gutsy thing to do. The family had asked the local shelters what they needed the most; the people in charge said, "Underwear," and, even at the risk of being known as "The Underwear Kid" for many years into the future — he did it.

Looking back and considering that I have spent hundreds of hours over the past many years following and studying Bar/Bat Mitzvah Mitzvah Projects, you will understand how difficult it is to keep all of the material organized. This should explain why the final section of this chapter is called **Random Thoughts, Reminders, And Wise Words From Other Bar/Bat Mitzvah People.**

Bear with me.

Consider this: You may actually be starting a trend that others around the community, the country, or the entire world will adopt. You do not have to be the first person in all of human history to come up with a specific project — though it is wonderful if you do, and many Bar/Bat Mitzvah Glorious *kinderlach* have. Just know that it *has happened* before.

As I said at the beginning and in the middle of this chapter, your project does *not* have to be Big Time. David Levitt got his school system to donate the leftover food from the cafeterias. Then he got the entire state of Florida to adopt it as a regular practice. He is now a student at the University of Florida, and the more than 1,000,000 pounds has been donated! I have a video from Nick News. David is about 15 years old at the time, and at the end he says, "If Pinellas County can collect 185,000 pounds of food by now, I think we can get millions of pounds." The first time I saw this, I said, "He's a nice young man, but he must be crazy!" *But,* he's already on his second million pounds, so *I* am the one who has to change my thinking about the Mitzvah power of Bar/Bat Mitzvah Mitzvah projects. Once again, though, the real message is that — if you are doing a food collection and manage to provide hungry people with 27 pounds or 123 pounds or 444 pounds of food — this makes a *huge* difference in the lives of many people. Pick one single bagel or doughnut shop or other food establishment and see how much you can accomplish. The website www.rockandwrapitup.org will be very useful for information about food collections. But *do* **think above and beyond.** It may be that you will actually achieve Big Time Tikkun Olam.

Don't be shy. In most situations your rabbi, teachers, cantor, synagogue, sisterhood, and men's club presidents, friends, merchants, food establishments, corporations and corporation CEOs, CFOs, CIOs, and just about anyone else will not only encourage you in your Mitzvah project, they will be happy to join in enthusiastically. If you want to ask the rabbi if it is all right to display flyers, brochures, or other materials about your Mitzvah project, or to place an attractive collection box or Mitzvah crib in the lobby, usually he or she will immediately agree. You may have doubts that he or she will agree. You might think your synagogue is too fancy to spoil the aesthetics of the lobby. Be prepared to be surprised. Just think of Rachel Margolin who belongs to a *very* big synagogue. She thought it would be a great idea to have the congregation allow her and her friends to dig up part of the lawn either at the main building or at the other education branch so the congregants could plant a Mitzvah Garden. They wanted to grow vegetables and donate them to a local soup kitchen. She got the idea from Marshall Levit from Houston, who created the first one in the Jewish community at Congregation Beth Jeshurun. (It was his Eagle Scout project.) Rachel met with the rabbi and the president of the congregation, and, yes, they loved the idea. Now here's the really good part — this wasn't even her Bat Mitzvah Mitzvah project. She did it when she was 9 years old! This is also a fine example of how, if you are a younger brother or sister, you don't have to wait. Some of these Mitzvah projects can be done by 9-year-olds, and younger.

And if you are an **older sister or brother,** you don't have to say, "Been there, done that!" Nor do you have to feel a sense of regret that you didn't do such a dazzling project for your own Bat or Bar Mitzvah. In either situation, you are most welcome to join your younger or older sibling in her or his project. Or, inspired by her or his Mitzvah project, you could launch another one of your own...no matter how old or young you are and no matter how well or badly you get along with your brother or sister in "regular" life. In *that* life, outside of the Mitzvah realm, you may be the kinds of kids who have to be separated in the car during a roadtrip because you are always fighting with each other. But this is different, and while it may not lead to peaceful relations every day, you have created a time warp and safe haven of Mitzvahs that allows for moments of *real* normalcy. In reality, the rest of "regular" life doesn't seem so normal to me. Otherwise, how would we explain why kids — who would never think to do dishes or straighten their rooms — clean toilets and scrub bathtubs and floors in a shelter because it is a Mitzvah to provide homeless or frightened people with a clean, Menschlich place to live?

The Bar/Bat Mitzvah Mitzvah project is, in a way, a revolution. As mentioned in the first chapter of this book, it is a very recent development in modern Jewish life, but it has taken hold, and beautifully so. The proof: One of our glorious *kinderlach* asked my student, teacher, and friend, Rabbi Neal Gold, "You mean there was a time when kids *didn't* do Mitzvah projects?"

As you can tell, I have been so psyched writing this section of the book, I have to end this chapter with four statements with exclamation marks:

Just Do It! Now begin your Real Live Journey into the Life of Mitzvahs. You will gain an authentic sense of what the Jewish concept שמחה של מצוה/Simcha Shel Mitzvah, The Joy of Doing Mitzvahs really means. You will certainly look back upon this venture with a sense of pride for the rest of your life.

Enjoy! Enjoy! — which is not exactly the same as the next line...

Have fun! If you read this book cover to cover, you won't be the first person who thinks, "Siegel's stuff is soooo serious, sooooo heavy! He must be a real downer/grump/whiner in person. Where's the fun?" I just wanted to make sure everyone knows that the author not only believes that you can have fun doing Mitzvahs, but also that, if you don't, you are, well, missing the fun. It's not *all* high-sounding, awesome cosmic stuff. So you heard it from me, myself, first — **Have Fun!**

לחיים/Lechaim - To Life!

Your Mitzvah Money

We make a living by what we get, but we make a life by what we give.
(Winston Churchill)

Giving Your Tzedakah Money Away Wisely: How You Can Make Miracles Happen

Money, money, *so much money* is all around you for the Bar/Bat Mitzvah. "Regular" money for expenses, and Mitzvah money to be given away to Tzedakah. This is a (forgive the pun) golden opportunity for everyone involved to gain a very real sense of these two distinct categories of money, and the power both have in their own realm to make things happen. It is a most appropriate time to teach your child about the meaning of the word **"investments."** Buying stocks and bonds is one kind of investment. Be sure to explain, though, that investments with Tzedakah money may mean something else more sublime. Remind them that the benefits may not be immediately apparent, but they are no less real than periodic dividend checks. In many ways, they are *more* real.

You may also want to stress that, according to Jewish tradition, **Tzedakah money never belongs to us.** (Numbers Rabba 5:2, Mishna Nedarim 11:3[13], and other texts) It *always* belongs to the beneficiary, and our responsibility — as awesome as it sounds — is to serve as God's שליחים/Shelichim, Mitzvah Messengers to distribute it wisely. In this capacity, we are commanded to distribute the Tzedakah money to its rightful owners.

There is an extremely important concept we have to keep in mind: Because Tzedakah money never belongs to us, the people in need are *entitled* to receive what is given to them. Just as in the United States, for example, the Americans with Disabilities Act *entitles* certain individuals to Braille signs, ramps, elevators that beep at every floor, and many other adjustments. We *owe* it to them. It *belongs* to them. The person performing the Mitzvah of Tzedakah is not doing the other person a favor, and the situation is not defined as one of "helper" and "helpee." Someone "needs," someone else "has," and the one who "has" adjusts the imbalance by sharing with the one who "needs." In my opinion, this elevates the level of giving beyond the common understanding of *voluntarily* using our money for the common good. For example, just knowing that someone who could not afford a Passover Seder can sit and enjoy like a free person just like everyone else *because* we used our Tzedakah money to make it happen, *because* it is the right thing to do is as high a human value as anyone could want. And this includes the same four cups of wine as everyone else.

This would also be an excellent opportunity to explain that Jewish tradition teaches that there are **two very distinct Mitzvahs** concerning the concept and reality of giving. The first one is "גְּמִילוּת חֲסָדִים/Gemilut Chassadim," giving of yourself, your volunteer time. The other is צְדָקָה/Tzedakah, in its more restricted sense, means using money to do Tikkun Olam. Both Mitzvahs make the world a better place, and both make human lives more Menschlich, but they solve problems in their own way, and both often work together to repair the world.

As you begin to do your research on where to distribute your Tzedakah money, you will soon discover that there is a vast variety of people in need. Jewish tradition teaches that (Leviticus Rabba [Margoliot] 34:6) "שבעה שמות נקראו לו עני אביון מסכן רש דל דך מך/There are seven different terms for poor people." "Seven" is a round number in Midrashic language. It means "several, many." "Poor people," of course, may be understood to include many different types of people who have needs — real food, heat, clothing, a job, companionship, safety from violence...*anyone* with *any* real needs.

There are different possible sources of your money Tzedakah money. You may decide to give away a portion of the money you receive as gifts. Or you may say to family and friends that you would prefer not to receive gifts, but instead, would ask them to support a particular Tzedakah project that is important to you. *(See below for details for the appropriate procedure. There is a catch.)* A Bat/Bar Mitzvah who decides to do this still usually gets presents. Not as many as others, but still, many people wish to do both for the Bar/Bat Mitzvah — donate *and* also give a gift.

There are also many ways to distribute your Tzedakah money wisely. You may decide to use some of it to purchase various items which you then donate to appropriate recipients in need. If you do so, you need to remember two things: (1) When you go to the store to buy the Mitzvah items, take a letter from your Rabbi or teacher that explains exactly what you are doing, i.e., that your purchases are Mitzvah-purchases. (2) Always ask to speak to the manager or store owner. Explain what you are doing. The manager or owner will often donate extra items or give a significant discount because you are doing such a fine Mitzvah.

In addition, your community, synagogue, or school may have a program in which members of a particular year's Bar/Bat Mitzvah class pools donations from the entire class, and at the end of the year, the class decides to whom to give it. This often involves thousands of dollars and is a *very* exciting venture. Other options exist which allow for ongoing *group* Tzedakah activities, such as Washington, DC's, Jewish Youth Philanthropy Institute [www.jypi.org] and the B'nai Tzedek Program [www.hgf.org].

Just remember that, however you choose to distribute your Tzedakah money, use your intelligence, dreams, ideas, creativity, and all your other God-given gifts to have this Mitzvah money do Tikkun Olam. And try to do it in a way that you will always remember *what* you did and *how* you did it. We use our intelligence, dreams, ideas, creativity, and all our other God-given gifts in other areas of our lives. We should certainly apply them at least equally enthusiastically and creatively when it comes to Tzedakah. In my personal opinion, nothing in life compares to the power of Mitzvah money. No form of human personal satisfaction and pride can equal our personal feeling of accomplishment when we have done miracles with our minds, hearts, and souls…and Tzedakah. Some would say this is why we are given the Gift of Life. I would agree, and once you have felt it in your bones through your own acts of Tzedakah, you, too, might share that feeling.

The Two Absolutely Most Important Rules Concerning How and Where to Donate Your Tzedakah Money

The First Rule of Donating: No matter where you decide to donate, you must do some research to find out if they are following "The Three E's" — are they using their money *efficiently* and *effectively*, and are they using it *exactly* as they say they are using it. The first step is to get a copy of their budget. If it appears to you that they are spending too much money on administration and fundraising or that they are inefficient in other ways, *don't* give to them. There are other places where your money can make a bigger difference in the lives of other people. If the budget you receive is too complicated to understand, ask them to explain. Again, if the explanations do not satisfy you, do *not* give to them. Jewish tradition is very emphatic about this, as Maimonides states it in his 8 Levels of Tzedakah: One should not contribute to a Tzedakah fund unless the donor knows that the director is trustworthy and intelligent and knows how to manage the money properly. *(Mishna Torah, Laws of Gifts to Poor People, Chapter 10)*

Since you want to make sure that as much of your Mitzvah money is actually used for the Mitzvah, you will have to ask yourself what percentage of a Tzedakah project's money is acceptable for fundraising and administration expenses? (This is known as "overhead.") My personal opinion is that no more than 15% should be allowed, though in some very specific situations up to 20% is acceptable. Be aware, though, that there are many others who consider it acceptable to spend a much higher percentage on overhead. A friend recently showed me a very clever one-liner: *No one ever went out of business for having low overhead.* I, for one, would definitely *not* want 35¢ or 30¢ of every dollar I donate to not be used for the Mitzvah work that needs to be done. I am frequently astonished at how often people who make wise investments for themselves make some very bad Tzedakah decisions.

Don't be discouraged if the first Tzedakah organization or group you wanted to give to doesn't meet your standards. Keep looking. For example, if you want to make a difference about feeding hungry people, there are *many* worthy Mitzvah heroes and their *chevras*/organizations who are doing it just right. They are making certain that as much of your Mitzvah money is used to provide good, nutritious, and even fun food for people who cannot afford to buy enough food for the day, or week, or month. You *will* find the right one. Jewish tradition (Bava Batra 9b) explicitly teaches that you can proceed with confidence in your quest to do fine Tikkun Olam with your Tzedakah money:

ואמר רבי יצחק.....
כל הרודף אחר צדקה
הקדוש ברוך הוא ממציא לו מעות ועושה בהן צדקה
רב נחמן בר יצחק אמר
הקדוש ברוך הוא ממציא לו בני אדם המהוגנים
לעשות להן צדקה

Rabbi Yitzchak said...:
The Holy One will provide sufficient Mitzvah money
for any who runs to do Tzedakah.
Rabbi Nachman Bar Yitzchak said:
The Holy One will provide appropriate recipients
through whom to perform the Mitzvah of Tzedakah.

With that extra time and effort you put into it, you will certainly find it. A couple of simple comparisons should make this abundantly clear: (1) Just think about all the time people spend checking out every detail before buying a new car. (2) Consider high school seniors researching different colleges. It is important, of course, to buy a car which suits your personal needs. And it is even more important in the grand scheme of Life to pick the right college. Personally, I would think that, since Tzedakah money is such an awesome Mitzvah, we ought to devote our best talents to making the right decisions. The wellbeing of other people, and sometimes their very lives, depends on it.

The Second Rule is specific to Bar and Bat Mitzvah (and other life-cycle events): If you are asking others to donate to a specific project in your honor, *do **not** have them write checks directly to the project.* Rather, have them write the checks directly to you. This is the reasoning: For ethical reasons, the Tzedakah project does not tell the family *how much* each person gave. The result is that when friends and relatives give directly to the project, they often give much less than if they write the check directly to you. *That's* the catch I mentioned above in section 1:B. If you want to have more Tzedakah money to distribute, it is best to follow this procedure.

Finally, there is no absolutely "correct" answer to the question, **"Should I give it all in one place?** Or should I spread the Tzedakah around many Mitzvah heroes and projects?" If you do your research well, you will soon realize that there are situations where $23 can change a life, while $1,000 may have very little impact. A classic case is the Harvard University Endowment Fund. At one time the Endowment Fund was worth $13 billion. When I read an article about this enormous project, I thought, "If someone said he or she wanted to give $1,000,000, I would think it would be an unwise Tzedakah investment." I may be naïve and may not understand the nature of Big Numbers, but, I would think $1,000,000 could do much more world-fixing if it were used in other places. And at the very opposite end of the Tikkun Olam Impact Scale, for a few pennies, some Mitzvah heroes can provide life-saving medicines.

If you do your homework, you will be much better prepared to decide how and where your Mitzvah money will make a massive impact on the lives of many people. The research is no harder than preparing to write a paper on the War of 1812 for school. In fact, often it is much easier, *and,* more important I believe, the stakes are much higher than getting an A on a history paper.

The Buying Power of Your Tzedakah Money — Ask for a Wish List

Every Tzedakah project has specific things *they* need the most. They may be things like equipment and supplies, projects to be funded, such as scholarships for training, or transportation costs so individuals can participate in programs.

One example of a wish list should make this extremely clear: A woman in Jerusalem named Barbara Silverman founded an organization called A Package from Home which prepares and delivers packages to Israeli soldiers on the front lines and at their base. As of April, 2004, with volunteer help, she had assembled and delivered more than 55,000 of these packages. She *always* needs supplies, everything from M&M's (a favorite of the soldiers), t-shirts, long underwear, batteries, etc. Ask her for *her* wish list of what she needs. The needs vary depending (1) on the season, (2) what may be in especially short supply, or (3) what new item may have just-that-very-moment come to mind that she hadn't thought of until you asked. And, in addition, you should be aware that every package has a personal note enclosed, so you can have your friends and family write notes as part of your party-event. How you get the supplies to Israel is covered in another section of this book. Go to A Package from Home's website for more details: www.apackagefromhome.org.

Now, imagine yourself going into a store to buy something for yourself. Imagine that you have a big wad of cash in your pocket or a credit card with plenty of money in the bank to cover whatever you spend. And imagine that you may be thinking to yourself, "Ooooooh, I want this! I want that!" as you cruise the counters and displays. It's both the same and different when you are using your Tzedakah money to pay for items on a Mitzvah hero's or project's wish list. What is similar is that you should be at least as enthusiastic for this kind of shopping as for your own — something on the order of, "Ooooooh, I want this for them! I want that for them!" *But* it should feel like a different kind of "Ooooooh!" It *is* different — a different order of "up" feeling. *Because it is a Mitzvah,* it should feel absolutely terrific.

Giving Secretly

There are many reasons to donate Tzedakah money in such a way that the recipient does not know who gave the money. The most important reason is to save the recipient from any sense of embarrassment or shame. *And* there are many kinds of situations where doing it secretly is preferred. (See my translation of Maimonides' 8 Levels of Tzedakah at the end of the book.) Two examples: You may wish to provide the money for a Bar/Bat Mitzvah whose family cannot afford to have an appropriate Simcha. Or, you may have heard of Jewish Elders living in the Former Soviet Union who have very little money...not enough to have decent, nutritious food to carry them through the month. You do your research and find a group that delivers food packages to the Elders, but you don't need any acknowledgements. You just want to know that you have done the Mitzvah and that "somewhere in a land far, far away" people will not go hungry.

There are two excellent ways to do this. The first is through your Rabbi's Discretionary Fund. **Many** rabbis have what is known as a discretionary fund. This means that he or she receives Tzedakah money and may use it as he or she deems most appropriate for various needs. If you tell the rabbi, "Here are X number of dollars. I would like you to serve as my שליח/Shaliach, my Mitzvah Messenger." Then *you* tell the rabbi which specific Mitzvah you would like to make happen. You may be certain that it will be done. You will never know who benefited from your Tzedakah money, and the person enjoying the Bar/Bat Mitzvah and the Elder thousands of miles away who will eat well will not know who you are...but *you* will have the satisfaction of knowing you did a Big Time Mitzvah.

The second possible way you can distribute Tzedakah money privately, you will have to develop on your own. As you build your Mitzvah connections and do your research, you may find a trustworthy individual other than the rabbi who is always doing fine Mitzvahs. That person, your שליח/Mitzvah Messenger may very well be able to arrange it for you. One example, The Rabbanit Bracha Kapach provides for many Bar/Bat Mitzvah families in Israel. This includes nice clothes for the Bar/Bat Mitzvah, a lovely ceremony, Tallit and Tfillin, and food for a reception. As for the Elders in Moscow or Leningrad — many individuals are doing just that: providing food packages. In this area of Tikkun Olam, Igor Feldblyum's Am Echad organization is an excellent resource. [www.amechad.net] Also, go to www.ziv.org for a more complete description of the Rabbanit's work, and for more information about special agents in additional areas of Tikkun Olam.

A particularly fine touch is donating your Tzedakah money in honor of your parents, grandparents, other family members, Torah teachers, friends, and other individuals who have been especially important in your life. You may also want to give in memory of those who have passed away who played a major role in your life. This is one meaning of the verse in The Book of Proverbs (10:2): וּצְדָקָה תַּצִּיל מִמָּוֶת - And Tzedakah saves from death. One of the well-known interpretations is exactly this: Even after someone has left this life, what that person has taught you has the power to save other people's lives.

And an excellent follow-up: One Glorious Bat Mitzvah Kid issued a report to all those who donated. She summarized how her Mitzvah money was ultimately used, complete with pie charts and other wonderful graphics. Today, computer programs have become so simple, you can design a beautiful statement, complete with a personal message, for those who shared in your Mitzvah giving.

Special Situations

You may have a very personal connection to a particular type of Tzedakah project. The following are just a few examples of special situations, and how you may decide to approach supporting such projects with your Tzedakah money:

1. Because of a family member's or friend's **illness,** you may feel especially motivated to donate to some project that relates to care and cure for people affected by disease. One option is to publicize and donate to a worthy group or Mitzvah hero's work in Israel. In North America, there are four little-known, but incredibly powerful, projects that you may want to consider: Songs of Love [www.songsoflove.org], Books, Bears & Bonnets [www.booksbearsbonnets.org], Casting for Recovery [www.castingforreovery.org], and Hosts for Hospitals [www.hosts-forhospitals.org]. In addition to the difference your Tzedakah money will make, publicizing their Mitzvah work will bring great benefit to many more people.

B'nai and B'not Mitzvah are often determined to do Big Time Tikkun Olam, and they use their determination and creativity to make it happen. Two such individuals, Rachel Steigerwald of Edison, NJ, and Ben Goldhaber of Raleigh, NC, accepted the challenge of Making a *Big* Difference and produced extremely impressive results.

Rachel Steigerwald, of Metuchen, NJ, holds a teddy bear from one of the boxes she created for the Books, Bears & Bonnets program she established at Robert Wood Johnson Hospital, New Brunswick, NJ, as her Bat Mitzvah Mitzvah Project.

Rachel had learned about Books, Bears & Bonnets [BB&B], a project that provides a lovely, colorful box containing an age-and-gender-appropriate book, a cap, a teddy bear, a personal note and some other items to outpatients undergoing cancer treatments. Founded by Merrily Ansell of Bethesda, MD, the program was well integrated into most of the Washington and Baltimore area hospitals. It is truly a simple and effective project that should be in hospitals everywhere. However, Merrily is not free to travel around to introduce, explain, and set it up in other cities. Enter Rachel Steigerwald…as it were, a mere "kid." She did her homework. She learned all about BB&B, contacted

Merrily, and selected Robert Wood Johnson Hospital in New Brunswick, NJ, as a likely site to establish the program. It is a *very* big and famous hospital, but Rachel was not intimidated. She found a physician, Dr. Michael Nissenblatt (mentioned elsewhere in this book for his own Mitzvah work). He immediately understood the importance of Books, Bears, & Bonnets, and advised her, and directed her to the right people in the administration. As Rachel recently wrote, "It is very important to talk to the right person." Now, 200 miles away from where Merrily lives, the program flourishes, all because of Rachel's insight, research, and efforts.

Ben's story is especially moving. Diagnosed with cancer at age 7, his outpatient treatments at the hospital included sitting in a room with eight chairs and a video screen. The video allowed the children a few hours of distraction while the chemicals were being pumped into their bodies. The problem was that not everyone wanted to watch the same video. In that hospital, the only other available option was to be in a room where there was no video, no music, or any other entertainment-type diversions.

Ben Goldhaber of Raleigh, NC, holding some of the DVDs which he donated for use in the DVD players he donated to the children's outpatient cancer ward. Ben, a cancer survivor, just knew *that each child getting his or her chemothrapy treatment wanted to watch a video he or she chose.*

Ben's brilliant idea — which in retrospect is a real "Duh!" — was to provide individual DVD players and a selection of DVDs for each seat. It was an idea he got from his orthodontist's office where, while they are working on you, you can watch your own *individual* movie. A brilliant idea, yes, but very expensive. There is lots of good news, though. Ben is cured, significantly past the 5-year point, *and* after writing to electronics companies, canvassing local stores, raising money through his own campaign, he periodically delivers more and more DVD players and movies. Mitzvah Mission accomplished.

But there's even more good news: The children particularly like the privacy of having the earphones and the chance to focus on their own screens. It blocks out everything unpleasant about what is happening to their bodies.

And more: Personnel working in the adult areas of the hospital saw what Ben had done and decided to do the same for their patients. On the one hand, it is an even bigger "Duh!", and, on the other hand, it is just one more example of a child's Mitzvah-creativity serving as a model for the adult community. Cancer remains as difficult a trial to the human being as ever, but Rachel's (and Merrily's) and Ben's kinds of Tikkun Olam make for a very profound רפואת הנפש/Refu'at

HaNefesh, a cure for the human soul.

And just as I was writing this section about Ben's fabulous Mitzvah project, The following e-mail arrived from his mother, Susan:

Danny, I thought you'd appreciate this story. Today I got a call from the clinic where Ben was treated and where he donated the DVDs to. It was the head nurse and she wanted to tell me that they have had the newspaper article on Ben's DVD project posted on the bulletin board and one of the children being treated saw it and wanted to do something similar so he bought (or got contributed, the nurse wasn't sure) 3 DVD players and contributed them to the clinic. The nurse was calling us because the clinic really didn't need all 3 and the boy was very firm that we should check with Ben about what to do with the extras. So Ben said to give them to another clinic or part of the hospital that needs them. It was very gratifying.

Sincerely, Susan Goldhaber

My reply was rather simple, "Wow wow wow!" (And of course, "Yasher Koach!")

2. For too many reasons to count, you may want to have your Tzedakah money make an impact on the people living in **Israel.** There are so many possibilities. We believe that the best approach is to locate a Mitzvah hero who is doing direct, immediate Tikkun Olam. Go to www.ziv.org for dozens of possibilities. If, after surfing the Ziv website, you need further assistance developing a project, send an e-mail to ZivTzedaka@aol.com.

3. You may be an **animal person.** If so, the greatest resource I know that has everything anyone needs to learn about Mitzvahs relating to human-animal interaction is Delta Society. They are the best place to begin. [www.deltasociety.org.] I have included an endnote from Delta's source material entitled **Healthy Reasons to Have a Pet.** It is a fabulous list which can help you explain your human-animal Mitzvah project to others[14].

   A. If you are a **horse person,** consider giving to the Israel National Therapeutic Riding Association (INTRA). Anita Shkedi and her INTRA instructors and volunteers work miracles with people with every imaginable kind of disability. You can buy a horse — as Lisa Easton of Chevy Chase, MD, did — provide scholarships for riders unable to pay for lessons, buy saddles, bridles, and helmets, buy a year's supply of feed. There are many possibilities. [www.intra.org.il.]

   B. If you are a **cat or dog person,** consider supporting the incredible work of Avshalom Beni's Animal Assisted Therapy (AAT) in Israel. The name of his organization gives you a good idea of the kind of Tikkun Olam that Avshalom does: HAMA (ISRAEL) - <u>H</u>umans and <u>A</u>nimals in <u>M</u>utual <u>A</u>ssistance in Israel/

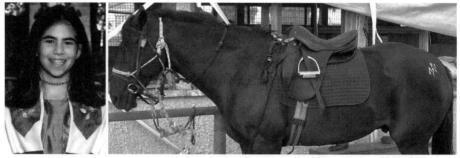

Lisa Easton, who used some of her Bat Mitzvah money to purchase Smokey,
The Mighty Mitzvah Horse, for the Israel National Therapeutic Riding Association.

חיות מחמד והאדם בסיוע הדדי בישראל With his Mitzvah cats and dogs, Avshalom works miracles with troubled families, individuals with emotional and mental difficulties, prisoners, and other people in need of this special kind of therapy. Contact Avshalom at hama-israel@bezeqint.net.

One Bat Mitzvah paid for a security system for Avshalom's cats and dogs. A would-be thief had cut through the fence and was going to steal these very valuable therapy animals. It may sound like a fairy tale, but, just in the nick of time, a Kid wanting to do something with animals inquired, the connection was made, and Keekee, Doobie, LaBelle, Chanel, and all the other Mitzvah cats and dogs are now safely out of the clutches of some dastardly individual. They are ready to continue doing their miracles under Avshalom's wise guidance.

This would also be a good opportunity for you to talk to your veterinarian about whether or not your own darling little Fang or Kelev or Bowser would be suitable for visits to nursing homes, hospitals, shelters, or schools. It might just be time for your kitty who sleeps 19 hours a day and your hound who just lounges around to get out there and start doing Mitzvahs.

C. If you are a **bird person,** you can buy birds and donate them to a local nursing home. They are colorful and fill the home with cheerful sound. They are not just for public areas, but should also be placed in the residents' rooms if they want them. The therapeutic value — the life-lengthening value — of caring for a bird (or cat or dog) has been proven in literally hundreds of scientific studies.

D. As for Mitzvah Nemo — if you are a **fish person,** you can purchase an aquarium and tropical fish for a shelter, an activities center for Elders, or a nursing home.

4. Finally, if you are a **plant person,** you can purchase plants and give them to residents in nursing homes to take care of. It makes a differ-

ence, a big difference. In fact, two important psychologists, Dr. Ellen J. Langer of Harvard University, and Dr. Judith Rodin, President of the University of Pennsylvania for a decade, did a wonderful study about plants in nursing homes. You don't really have to be an expert in the field to figure out some of the results. As Professor Anita Stewart of The Institute for Health & Aging and the Department of Social and Behavioral Sciences at the University of California, San Francisco summarized Langer's and Rodin's project, "The nursing home residents who were given a plant to take care of were more physically active and mentally alert." It is almost a "Duh!" conclusion. As long as a person has some one, even some thing to take care of, that person has a reason to go on living, to get up in the morning, to do something that has meaning. But there were more astonishing, measurable results. Professor Stewart continues, "But most dramatic of all was the fact that 18 months later, the residents in the 'responsibility enhanced' group had a mortality rate only half that of the control group." These are real "Wow!" results. For B'nai/B'not Mitzvah, buying plants and giving them to nursing home residents to care for is easy to do and truly awesome. Imagine, increasing the odds for someone to live longer by such a simple process! And, of course, you will want to continue to visit the Elder to see how the plant is doing, and how the Caregiver of the Holy Plant is thriving.

Israel

srael — vibrant, unique homeland, Holy Land, refuge for millions, central wellspring of the Jewish People's history. Whether in high times or hard times, under attack or at peace, visiting Israel and supporting Israel in as broad a variety and in the most creative ways is of supreme importance.

I can think of no better way to set the tone for this chapter than to quote my Torah teacher, teacher in Mitzvahs, student, and friend, Rabbi Neal Gold. In his 2003 Kol Nidray sermon, he told the congregation, *"When I was growing up, I always trusted my Hebrew school teachers. I trusted them, and I believed what they taught me. One thing I believed them about was what they told me about our relationship to Israel. They taught me that we loved Israel. They didn't say we "feel good about Israel," or that we "like the idea of Israel very much." They said: We love Israel."*

To this we must add comments by the distinguished Tanach/Bible scholar, Professor Jacob Milgrom in his explanation to Leviticus 19:18, "וְאָהַבְתָּ לְרֵעֲךָ כָּמוֹךָ/Love others as you love yourself." Professor Milgrom writes that the verb "אהב/A-H-V" "signifies not only an emotion or attitude, but also deeds." In other words, as Rabbi Gold explained further in his sermon, by saying that we *love* Israel it is not enough to just *feel* something in our minds, hearts, and souls. We have to *do* certain things to demonstrate what this love means.

Here, then, are a number of practical suggestions to make Israel part of the Bar/Bat Mitzvah experience. The general principle to guide you is, whatever you are considering for the Simcha, always ask, "Is there some way to relate this to Israel, the people, the Land, the needs for today and into the future?"

Go to Israel

The single most important thing a Bar/Bat Mitzvah family can do for Israel is, quite simply to go. Parents: **Go to Israel with your child.** Take your family, your extended family, your Tanta Chana who has never been in all her 79 years, and everyone else who might want to join you. And, yes, it's OK, and no, it isn't corny to ride around with your family and friends in a big tour bus that says on a gigantic banner, "Rosenbaum Bar Mitzvah Tour." It's just fine. Even better: Buy the Israel "I CARE AND I'M GOING" t-shirts for everyone who will join you. Often, there can also be a direct relationship between your child's Mitzvah project and the trip, as was true with a recent phone call I received. The Mother called; the Bat Mitzvah is 10 or 11 months away, the family is going in three or four months to Israel; the daughter loves animals, specifically dogs, horses, and dolphins — did I have anything to suggest for the trip?

The Ultimate Bat Mitzvah Mitzvah Israel Trip: Shira Papir and her family of Miami, Florida, wanted, above all else, two things to commemorate her Bat Mitzvah—the first was to celebrate it in Israel and the second was to make it a true Mitzvah mission.

With 22 family members in tow, ages 2 to 76 (12 adults and 10 kids), the Papir, Wolf and Fiske families departed for Israel with 20 extra duffels filled with T-shirts, small toiletries and 90 lbs of M&Ms for the soldiers, tons of baby clothes new and slightly used, children's books, perfumes, watches, stuffed animals, beanie babies, children's games, arts and craft supplies, school supplies, wedding dresses, dozens of packages of new socks for babies and children, infant toys, new towels, used eye glasses, and loads of dental supplies—tooth brushes, floss, toothpaste, cases of latex gloves. And, finally, nearly $5,000 in Tzedakah money to be given away as the needs were discovered. All of these items had been graciously donated by other family and friends.

Along with traditional touring sites, the whole *mishpacha*-family had the chance to visit and hand deliver all of the Mitzvah items to Dental Volunteers in Israel, the Rabbanit Kapach, Shaare Zedek Hospital where they had Sivan the Mitzvah Clown join them as they visited sick children, Barbara Silverman to whom they gave all of the items for the soldiers, tour Shalva, packed up and delivered goodie bags for the Egged bus drivers in Jerusalem (including letters from Shira's 5th and 6th grade classmates) shopped for needed items to be given to survivors of terror attacks and finally held a pizza party with soldiers at a tank base in the North — something the entire family agreed was the highlight of the trip! (The happiest person was the pizzeria owner — 70 pizzas were delivered that day!) This is a perfect example of Israel experience with the Bat/Bar Mitzvah Mitzvah Project. Shira and her family have set a wonderful precedent for others.

There really is **no need to justify _why_ you should go to Israel.** I have always found it curious that no one ever asked the Kennedys, "Why are you going to Ireland?" So why would we have to explain or apologize for a trip like this? Even less is there a need to explain why everyone should go _now_ when Israel and Israelis are being so violently assaulted. At various times in our lives we all need to live with our fears, deal with them, and then do something about them. We have done it after the terror of September 11th, though in Israel it is worse, and a much more frequent occurrence. And we deal with our fears in other areas of our lives, which is one reason why I feel we should be doing it no less when it relates to Israel.

I think Rabbi Irvin Wise of Cincinnati said it best when he advertised a forthcoming congregational tour of Israel. He invited his congregants to join him on a "Not If Family Mission to Israel." Rabbi Wise was countering the all-too-frequent reactions, "If the situation gets better, I'll go." To Rabbi Wise (and the many congregants who signed up for the tour), you don't wait, you just go.

It may even be that there are some parents who hear a whispered, powerful thought in the back of their minds. It keeps coming up again and again. It's when the child asks, "Abba, Eema, what were you doing when...?" In the context of your child becoming a Mitzvah Person, what better message could you transmit to your child than to take your daughter or son with you to Israel? And if you want to be more "extreme," you may even consider going for a longer stretch of time, an entire summer, or, with Sabbatical time for some people, an entire year. You will not be the first ones to do it. You will also not be the first ones to have reaped the benefits for years and years to come, benefits for parents and children, and parents-and-children as a family alike.

This is more than a trip or a vacation. It is *your* pilgrimage back to *your Jewish roots,* a strengthening of identity, an opportunity to get a new, refreshing perspective of what it is to be Jewish, to be alive, and to be alive-and-Jewish.

There are also many options for **paying for the trip.** Some families decide not to have a big party or reception, and to use that money instead for the bringing the family to Israel. Many set aside some of the money saved to be used as Tzedakah money. This is a very old Jewish tradition based on the Talmudic statement (Pesachim 8b):

אמר רבי אלעזר
שלוחי מצוה אינן ניזוקין לא בהליכתן ולא בחזירתן

Rabbi Elazar said, "People going on a Mitzvah-mission will not be harmed, neither on the way to do the Mitzvah nor on the way back."

Some families that can afford it, do both the trip *and* a reception or party. And if, as has been true in a few family situations, you can make a stopover in your ancestors' cities, towns, or villages, so much the more powerful will be the experience.

Whatever fits your family's situation, however, whenever — in any event, go to Israel and bring as many people with you as you possibly can.

Many and Varied Options

In several other sections of this book, I make reference to the Bar/Bat Mitzvah Event and Israel, including donating Tzedakah money to worthy Mitzvah heroes and Mitzvah projects in Israel, collecting and sending items needed for Mitzvah projects in Israel with someone travelling over [go to www.ziv.org for specific items to bring], and letter-writing and caring-note-writing activities with your guests to many segments of the Israeli population who need to hear that we care. Particularly because Israel and Israelis feel abandoned by the media and so many governments around the world, it is ever-so-important that they know they are not alone.

There are many options for **buying products made in Israel.** For example, beyond the famous Israeli wines, the number of food products available locally (literally from soup to nuts) grows every day. Then there are gift items for relatives and friends — CDs, DVDs, videos, books, posters, prints, t-shirts, Ahava and other cosmetic and skin products, ritual objects such as Tzedakah boxes, Seder plates, *dreidels,* and Hanukkah Menorahs of every possible design and price range. There are also many possibilities for the physical lay-out of the events: tablecloths, decorations, other items necessary for the sanctuary, dining areas, and other physical spaces. This is the very short list.

There are several ways to make the purchases: You can buy from Mitzvah projects that make a tremendous number of beautiful articles for yourself and/or to give to others, and you can buy from merchants whose businesses have been hard hit by the economic problems resulting from the recent years of terror. Another option: Your mind will spin if you visit a local store that sells Israeli products. And finally, the old 21st Century stand-by…30 seconds on the Web will provide so many other items for purchase, you will be dazzled…all of them to buy with a simple click of the mouse.

Even more opportunities exist for **families working on a big budget.** Because of the many articles in newspapers and magazines about grotesquely lavish affairs, some people are deceived into thinking that *everyone* has huge sums of money to spend on the Bar/Bat Mitzvah. This is simply not so, but this paragraph is intended for those families that *do* have a lot of money at their disposal. A few opportunities to spend *many Mitzvah-dollars* include: (1) taking care of the needs of hundreds of people in Israel; (2) establishing a scholarship fund for youth and adults to go to Israel; (3) and paying the bills for a Mitzvah hero for six months, a year, or any stretch of time so that she or he can concentrate on Mitzvahs rather than having to worry about raising money to keep doing dazzling Tikkun Olam.

Especially interesting is one very special project, as explained to me by my friend, Louise Cohen. She suggests that, in honor of the Bar/Bat Mitzvah, a family could take out an advertisement about Israel in a local or national newspaper. Many such ads cover media bias, such as newspapers that never use the word "terrorist" when Israelis are murdered in cafés, on buses, in their homes. Louise mentioned another topic that caught my attention. To quote her e-mail, it was *"one which documents the hate education in the Palestinian (and other Arab) school books and kid's television shows. (And of the failure of the world media to acknowledge this abomination.) This is appropriate because Bar Mitzvah is the time when the family and guests are most conscious of educational landmarks, and the impact of early education and other experiences on an emerging young adult."* CAMERA, The Committee for Accuracy in Middle East Reporting in America, is a superb organization to help you with this kind of project. [www.CAMERA.org]

Helpful Techniques,
Tools and Short-Cuts

www.ziv.org, The Web, Google, E-mail and Mitzvahs

(By Arnie Draiman, With Additions By the Author)

www.ziv.org, Your Most Important Website

The web is an incredible resource for all aspects of the Bar/Bat Mitzvah as well as for many, many other things in Life. The key to www.ziv.org is in the name "זיו-Ziv," which means "radiance." I chose the name because (a) there is a certain radiance in the Mitzvah-act itself, and (b) the more I got to meet, know, and work with Mitzvah heroes, I recognized that there was a certain radiance to their presence. By joining them in their Mitzvah work, it is hoped that some of that זיו-Ziv, radiance rubs off on all of us. www.ziv.org lists more than 100 Mitzvah projects and Mitzvah heroes in Israel, the United States, and other parts of the world. These Mitzvah heroes and projects involve a huge variety of Tikkun Olam: our Elders, providing for people barely able to put food on the table, survivors of terrorist attacks and homicide bombers in Israel, individuals with disabilities, human-animal relations, kids doing marvelous Tikkun Olam,... to name just a few.

The Ziv Home Page: www.ziv.org

This page gives you the overview of what Ziv is and will have links to various parts of the website including our Annual Report, the Annual November Update, and other updates of people and places we fund; other books — like this one – that are available about Mitzvahs and Tikkun Olam in the section under "Books"; information on the Ziv-Giraffe Curriculum for schools (link: "Ziv Curriculum"); many unique things we are doing in Israel (like having pizza and schwarma parties for Israeli soldiers!) (link: "Direct Aid in Israel"); links to our favorite places, and more.

By the time you are reading this in print, the Ziv website might look a little different than explained here, but the basics will generally be the same. If not, we trust in you — the computer-savvy kids — to figure it out!

Some of the Inside Pages You Need to Know About

1. **The Ziv Annual Report:** The Annual Report, published every April, gives you an insight into every project and person we work with. It also includes direct contact information so you will be able to get in

touch with any of them. The Report is about 40 pages long, but don't be daunted. It is clearly divided into sections by topic, though many of the people and places we support fit into more than one category. So, to make it easier, you can use the Alphabetical listing of projects or the Geographical breakdown (which would help you locate which projects are in or near your own community, which ones are in Israel, etc.) Of course, the Annual Report is printed every year, so if you prefer, you can request a hard copy directly from Naomi Eisenberger at naomike@aol.com.

2. **The Ziv Annual November Update:** A much smaller version of the Annual Report, it is just what its name implies: an update of various events and developments that have taken place since April.

3. **Link: Bar/Bat Mitzvah Information: So You're Having a Bar/Bat Mitzvah?:** An excellent place to see and read information relating to the Big Event. Of course, much of that information is printed here in this book as well.

4a. **Israel Update (Link: Direct Aid to Israel):** There are various places on the website relating to Israel. You can see pictures and read about some of the incredible Mitzvah work we are doing in Israel: Mitzvah clowning; distributing teddy bears to sick children; giving out packets of sunflower seeds, nuts, and other snacks to Egged bus drivers with notes of caring and encouragement attached; delivering pizza to the IDF soldiers with personal cards from kids and adults from around the world, and more.

4b. **Opportunities for Direct Assistance in Israel:** This gives you very specific information about several Ziv projects and what their particular needs are. While the list is limited, we are willing to hear any and all suggestions that you — the great Mitzvah Person you are — might have.

There are, of course, links to all the projects that have websites. (Most do.) The links can be found throughout the Annual Reports (for all years), the November Updates, and on our Links page.

In addition, the Ziv website has various articles about Tzedakah and Tikkun Olam, regular updates on our activities in Israel, including what you specifically can do to make a difference, periodic information about Mitzvah heroes conferences in the United States, the annual Ziv HeroIsrael trip to Israel to meet these Giants of Tikkun Olam as they go about their awesome Mitzvah work, resources for teachers, and much, much more. (And you could create your own Bar/Bat Mitzvah Hero Trip too, whether to Israel or just visiting local Mitzvah Heroes!)

The Web, Google, and Mitzvahs

During my lectures, I often tell my audience that, if you get stalled on a project, find an 8-year-old, put her or him in front of your computer, and she or he will find what you need. Raised on URL, DSL, T-1, megabytes, gigabytes, and terabytes, digitalization, and firewalls; as familiar with RAM and ROM as the Romans were with Remus and Romulus; capable of communicating through a half-dozen instant messages simultaneously, unrattled by cyberspace and hyper-speed; a mindset accustomed to thinking in keywords, they know — they feel in their fingers — how a few seconds and a click on Google or some other search engine will fill the screen with The Right Stuff. It comes naturally to them. Even to the non-geeks among them.

Perhaps another way to look at this web work is that all of the information you want and need is there, just waiting for you to type in the right keywords and discover it. It reminds me of those little alien creatures in *Toy Story* clamoring about and saying "Choose me, choose me!"

If you or your family have a website, prominently post the story of your Bar/Bat Mitzvah Mitzvah project. And if you do *not* have your own, have the computer whiz-kid — you, yourself, if you can, or the proverbial 8-year-old — create one. There are plenty of free sites out in cyberspace, and a one-page proclamation of the Mitzvah project will be most welcome and will make a big difference! Once the website is up and running, let Ziv Tzedakah Fund know (www.ziv.org) and others, and the word will get out all over cyberspace.

A word to parents: Unless you are in the computer business, allow your Glorious Child to take you farther and faster in this research than you could do on their behalf. It will be a fine partnership, and there is no embarrassment in considering your child more advanced in this field than you are. So, after your family discussions of any and all topics relating to the Bar/Bat Mitzvah, let the younger generation do its thing and bring the Mitzvah web search results back to you. There are a number of other websites that cover Bar/Bat Mitzvah, including Mitzvah projects, and your child will no doubt find them with greater speed and ease than you could. You do not necessarily have to defer to your daughter or son about the conclusions she or he draws as a result of the research. *That* must always be open to discussion. But allowing your daughter or son to be the teacher in the process offers an additional advantage: It will demonstrate to your child ever-so-clearly that tools can be tools-for-Mitzvahs.

E-mail and Mitzvahs

As mentioned above regarding a website — if you choose to create one, e-mail can also be a terrific way to let the entire world know about your Mitzvah project. We have seen the power of e-mail in action. It is more powerful than you could possibly imagine. Here is what we suggest: Write an e-mail describing what you are doing, why you are doing it, what you need from those who will read the e-mail (do you need money?, items to be donated?, etc.), a little bit about yourself and where you live, go to synagogue, (people love to read that stuff), and be specific about how to be in touch with you. If you are looking for "things" to be donated, give them suggestions as to where they may best get such items....stressing that these are Mitzvah items.

Before you send it, read it again and make sure you have everything you need clearly stated. It should have all of the details, but do not include your telephone number or street address. (You never know who will see the e-mail somewhere down the line.) It shouldn't be too long, but it should cover everything you want to say. Do you want to add the infamous line "send this to everyone you know"? Be careful — because you don't want anyone to think it is spam, which they might automatically delete. You *do* want all the good people to read it and forward it on, so think twice about using that line. It is also a good idea to have someone else read it before you send it, proofreading for typos, adding an idea here or there, etc.

Why go through so much trouble to send one little e-mail? Because the power of the e-mail is that it can go from your computer to your friend's computer and then on and on to his and then to hers, etc. Within a very short period of time (a couple of days, a week, etc.) your e-mail can be all over the world and posted on all sorts of websites. Don't be surprised. This is the power of the internet.

And be sure to have your parents send it to all of their friends and family members. And be sure that your rabbi, cantor, youth director, teacher, etc. all get a copy as well.

Don't expect that everyone who reads it will respond. Many will read it and pass it on. Others will drop you a line and say "Yasher Koach." And then a few will actually respond with what you asked for. But those few are worth their weight in gold. Cyberspace is, indeed, a wonderful 21st Century way to spread the Mitzvah.

Lists to Make

The following is a review of some of the suggested lists and exercises mentioned in various parts of this book which may make the Bar/Bat Mitzvah more meaningful, with a few additional last-minute items. You are already making lists of invitees, who sits where, (and who absolutely must *not* sit next to whom), flight and train arrival times, what to bring to the synagogue before the Bar/Bat Mitzvah – all kinds of things. What I have added is meant to help you remember a different kind of "important things to remember," some of which should be considered and dealt with long before the Bar/Bat Mitzvah event itself. Add this list of lists to your already-growing list:

- What you want for yourself in Life. (Be very specific.)
- What you do *not* want for yourself in Life. (Be very specific.)
- What you *like* to do.
- What you *really* like to do.
- What you *don't* like to do, but might do if it were a fine Mitzvah to do.
- What you do well.
- What do you do *really* well.
- What you *don't* do well, but might do if it were a fine Mitzvah to do.
- Things that distress you that you would like to change, including all the wrong or bad reasons why some people are unhappy, suffer, or die.
- Things that are wrong in the world that you can change right now.
- Tikkun Olam-type things that you were always told were impossible to do but you have a sense that maybe they aren't *really* impossible.
- Mitzvah projects you already know are being done in your own community, or have heard about or read about that are happening elsewhere.
- 100 blessings in your life.

- A second list of 100 blessings in your life.
- Role models, goodhearted people, and Mitzvah heroes you know or have heard or read about.
- Individuals you want to honor in a special way on your Bat/Bar Mitzvah.
- People with "special" needs you know

    (a) who will be coming to the Bar/Bat Mitzvah,
    (b) whom you don't know, but who also might be coming to the Bar/Bat Mitzvah,
    (c) people with special needs that you know in other parts of your life.

- Synonyms for the word "Mensch."
- All the Hebrew, Yiddish, and Ladino terms that relate to Mitzvahs, Tzedakah, Tikkun Olam, and being a *Mensch.*
- The A-B-C's of Mitzvahs: Hyphenated words that start with "Mitzvah."
- The A-B-C's of Holiness: Common Objects, Acts, and Emotions Preceded By the Word "Holy."
- Super Mitzvah websites.
- Positive personality traits you would like to see in yourself.
- Negative traits you would like to remove from your personality.
- Things in Life That Are Priceless, Meaningful, to Be Cherished, and Prized Above All Else.
- Time lines comparing how much time was spent on making sure the Glorious Kid's skirt and blouse or suit is cleaned and pressed compared to discussing just exactly why having a Mitzvah project and donating to Tzedakah is so important,
  then *planning it and doing it*!!!

The A-B-C's of Mitzvahs
And The A-B-C's of Holiness

The A-B-C's of Mitzvahs

Almost any word can be combined with the word "Mitzvah" by using a hyphen. By making this compound word, you are endowing a common object with the potential to be used for Mitzvahs.

For example, "Mitzvah-sprinkles" on top of an ice-cream waffle cone may be given to a child who never gets a treat.

For example, a "Mitzvah-keyboard" is one used by a musician who takes the keyboard to people who are unable to go out of their homes. The musician takes an inanimate object, animates it with Mitzvahs by playing that person's favorite music. Or it could be a computer keyboard, if, for example, a Bat/Bar Mitzvah is showing Elders how to write their Life's story, compose e-mails, or use the internet.

For example, "Mitzvah-copies of Good Night Moon" are books given to children whose family cannot afford to buy them something lovely to read before they go to sleep.

When you think of it, it is simply awesome that any person has the power to take common objects, moments, or emotions, and to move them into a higher, more sublime realm.

Here is a list I composed. Almost everything came to mind in one sitting. Make your own list. Most of all, enjoy recognizing how much Mitzvah-potential there is all around us…everywhere.

A: Mitzvah-apple pie, Mitzvah-animal balloon tying tricks, Mitzvah-attitude, Mitzvah-air miles

B: Mitzvah-bottle, Mitzvah-banana

C: Mitzvah-Cadillac, Mitzvah-chip, Mitzvah-candle, Mitzvah-clowning, Mitzvah-credit, Mitzvah-copies of Good Night Moon

D: Mitzvah-dawg (I was raised in the South), Mitzvah-doodling, Mitzvah-digital photos, Mitzvah-dawn-walk-in-Jerusalem

E: Mitzvah-empty-chunky-tunafish-can, Mitzvah-eyeglasses

F: Mitzvah-flippers, Mitzvah-finch

G: Mitzvah-grocer, Mitzvah-gizmo

H: Mitzvah-horses, Mitzvah-hair-do

I: Mitzvah Israeli-flags, Mitzvah-Israel-air tickets, Mitzvah-internet

J: Mitzvah-joke, Mitzvah-job, Mitzvah-jelly beans,
  Mitzvah-jump rope, Mitzvah-jack-of-all-trades
K: Mitzvah-keyboard, Mitzvah-kite
L: Mitzvah-links, Mitzvah leftovers
M: Mitzvah-monster movies, Mitzvah-magician, Mitzvah-mango,
  Mitzvah-mouse, Mitzvah-Minnie Mouse dolls
N: Mitzvah-nose, Mitzvah-noodles
O: Mitzvah-oxygen mask, Mitzvah-operation
P: Mitzvah-pizza-parties for Israeli soldiers, Mitzvah-pacemaker,
  Mitzvah-pillowcases, Mitzvah-pick; Mitzvah-prom dresses
Q: Mitzvah-quilts, Mitzvah-(e)questrian therapeutic riding programs
R: Mitzvah-rides, rinks, and rings, Mitzvah-Rolls Royces,
  Mitzvah-(Merry-go)-rounds
S: Mitzvah-shekels, Mitzvah-search-engine, Mitzvah-string,
  Mitzvah-sox, Mitzvah-sprinkles
T: Mitzvah-trivia, Mitzvah-tango
U: Mitzvah-underwear, Mitzvah-ukuleles
V: Mitzvah-violins, Mitzvah-valedictorian
W: Mitzvah-watch
X: Mitzvah-(x)cappuccino cheesecake (the "x" is silent)
Y: Mitzvah-Yodels
Z: Mitzvah-zoo, Mitzvah-Ziesskeit

The A-B-C's of Holiness

I believe that the words "holy" and "holiness" have been sold short in American society, and in our Jewish upbringing and education. They are under-used. The words have been all-too-restricted to places like synagogues or certain books. I think that this is wrong, and that we can change it in the following way: By taking common objects, simple acts, emotions, or personality traits and using them for Mitzvahs, they acquire a certain holiness. As a result, we are taught an extremely important lesson: we, no matter who we are — old, young, male, female, exceptionally bright or of average or below-average [I dislike all those terms] intelligence have the power to bring more holiness into the world.

The actual meaning of the three-letter Hebrew root ק ד ש/K-D-Sh is "separate," "set apart," and from there to holy. We have available Mitzvah-opportunities, everywhere and at all times. We have the power to take things, experiences, and moments from the common realm, to set those common things, experiences, and moments apart and move all of them into the world of values and Tikkun Olam. Becoming a בר/בת מצוה - Bar/Bat Mitzvah-"Mitzvah Person" means the glorious *kinderlach* are moving into the full-time and Big Time world of holiness. This is what is meant by "Bar/Bat Mitzvah can be a transformative experience." Mitzvahs take us out of the world of negatives and neutrals, into a universe of positive, affirmative value-laden meanings.

Thus, an automobile tire becomes a holy automobile tire when it is purchased and donated to an individual whose livelihood depends on a car, is living in difficult financial circumstances, has a blow-out, and cannot afford to buy a new tire. By taking this tire from the realm of a "regular radial" it has become a Mitzvah tire, and has therefore entered the realm of the holy.

Another — classic — example is mentioned by my friend, Louis Berlin. When he teaches about Tzedakah, he will show his audience a holy document: a cash receipt for chickens purchased with Tzedakah money at Mr. Hacker's butcher shop so Clara Hammer, the Chicken Lady of Jerusalem, can provide chickens for poor people for Shabbat and holidays.

Human beings have that much power!

Now it is time to make another list, your own personalized list:

A: Holy automobile tires

B: Holy bicycles, Holy bloodmobiles

C: Holy cash receipts, Holy computer programs

D: Holy dreams

E: Holy e-mail, Holy Elvis records

F: Holy fingerprint and finger paints, Holy face painting and house painting

G: Holy glasses

H: Holy Hebrew newspapers, Holy hands

I: Holy irises, Holy individualism, Holy irrigation

J: Holy Jerusalem, Holy jalopies, Holy Jewish education

K: Holy kits and kitties

L: Holy logs, Holy licenses

M: Holy mud, Holy merry-go-round rides; Holy math tutoring

N: Holy Newman's Own All Natural salad dressings

O: Holy optical inventions

P: Holy paste and polish

Q: Holy questions, Holy quotations

R: Holy roofs

S: Holy soccer balls, Holy scalpels

T: Holy tea

U: Holy umbrellas

V: Holy vitamins, Holy vocational training

W: Holy washing machines, Holy windows

X: Holy xylophones, Holy X-rays, Holy (e)xtra-beautifully-wrapped presents for people who never get presents, Holy (e)xtraordinarily beautiful towels, sheets, and pillowcases

W: Holy Western Wall, Holy walkers, Holy websites

Y: Holy yearnings

Z: Holy zebra

85 of the Best Quotes You Will Ever Need For Your Bat or Bar Mitzvah Speech

(In no particular order, and with occasional comments in brackets by the author.)

*A*s anyone who has to give a speech knows, finding an absolutely-unforgettable quote is often the most difficult part of preparing. Sayings, aphorisms, and proverbs of all types and quality are big-ticket items, particularly for an often-already-nervous Bar/Bat Mitzvah who are often daunted by the task at hand. They may know exactly what they want to say based on their Torah portion; they may have even written down and rehearsed an astonishing and profound presentation. Still, they are looking for that extra "zing" element.

Many of their grandparents can still quote President Kennedy's inauguration line, which, paraphrased, goes something like this: "Ask not what your country can do for you. Rather, ask what you can do for your country." They heard this line decades ago, and they can still feel in their soul the thrill of those words and how it moved them to Tikkun Olam on a grand scale. Now, two generations later, the B'nai/B'not Mitzvah search, and, even with the help of the web, they sometimes come up empty handed. At best, they discover a one-liner or two-liner like "The early bird catches the worm" (which always made my stomach churn), or the one heard from earliest childhood, "An apple a day keeps the doctor away" — (which always fails to include that many apples in the store are coated with wax and whether or not organic apples are the only kind that are good for you). The down side of trying to squeeze great meaning into a few words is that, if it is said or heard enough times, we might conclude, "Well, yes, that's *sort of* true, but not totally." That is certainly the case with those clever bumper stickers we read when we stop at a traffic light.

So, partially-true and clever are nice, but not enough. It is the *content* of the full speech, what is derived from the words of Torah, that will carry the day. These can either highlight or stimulate your thinking and writing about the ideas you want to emphasize.

I offer the following list that I have collected to help ease the difficulties composing the speech. Almost all of them are brief and user-friendly. Nevertheless, they are meant only as points of departure or reinforcement for the deeper substance of the total message. Many of these are taken from Torah, Talmud, Midrash, and modern Jewish sources. Others come from everything from a food reviewer to people I couldn't even track down with the help of the all-holy search engines.

Please note, that since there are so many of them, there was no way to put them in any logical order, so please do skip around the list. Also, I have occasionally added some of my own comments in brackets, as well as translations and comments by my teachers and friends, in order to place the quotes in a Mitzvah/Tikkun Olam context.

I have also usually preserved "he" in the original quotes, though today we would say "he or she."

1.   החיים הם מצוות.
   Life is Mitzvahs. (*הרבנית*/ *The Rabbanit Bracha Kapach*)

2. To be is to do. (*Myriam Mendilow, ז"ל*)

3. Tzedakah is not about giving; Tzedakah is about being.
   (Rabbi Bradley Shavit Artson)

4.   אמר רבי אלעזר...שצדיקים אומרים מעט ועושים הרבה
   Rabbi Elazar Says:
   Tzaddikim-Good People say little and do much. *(Bava Metzia 87a)*

5. Nobody makes a greater mistake than he who does nothing because he could only do a little. *(Edmund Burke)*

6.   שמעון בנו אומר...
                     ולא המדרש הוא העקר אלא המעשה
   Shimon [the son of Rabban Gamliel] says:
   It is not what one says, but rather what one does,
   that makes all the difference in the world. *(Pirke Avot 1:17)*

7. To be is to stand for. *(Abraham Joshua Heschel, ז"ל)*

8. To be Jewish is to be an idealist. *(Unknown Source)*

9. To be is to be-with-dignity. *(Anonymous)*

10. Charismatic leaders make us think,
    "Oh, if only I could do that, be like that."
    True leaders make us think,
    "If they can do that, then...I can too." *(John Holt, Educator)*

11. When I was young, I admired clever people. As I grew old, I came to admire kind people. *(Abraham Joshua Heschel, ז"ל)*

12. Here is the test to find whether your mission on earth is finished. If you're alive, it isn't. *(Richard Bach)*

13.   אם תרצו, אין זו אגדה.
    If you will it, it is no fantasy. *(Theodore Herzl)*

14. Never doubt that a small group of thoughtful, committed citizens can change the world; indeed, it's the only thing that ever does.
    (Margaret Mead)

15. Realize that if you have time to whine and complain about something then you have the time to do something about it.

(Anthony J. D'Angelo)

16. Most of the things worth doing in the world had been declared impossible before they were done. *(Justice Louis Brandeis)*

17.

הוּא הָיָה אוֹמֵר

לֹא עָלֶיךָ הַמְּלָאכָה לִגְמוֹר.

וְלֹא אַתָּה בֶן חוֹרִין לִבָּטֵל מִמֶּנָּה.

(The usual translation):
Rabbi Tarfon used to say,
It is not incumbent upon you to finish the work,
but neither are you free to desist from it. *(Pirke Avot, Chapter 2)*

(My free translation):
In your own lifetime, you may not finish all the Mitzvah work that needs to be done, but that is not a sufficient reason for not digging in and doing everything possible within your human and Jewish power to Fix the World.

[By a slight change in which word is italicized, there can be two valid interpretations of Rabbi Tarfon's intent: (1) Do something! or (2) Do something! Both are important ways to respond to the need to do Tikkun Olam.]

18. A mind once stretched by a new idea never regains its original dimension. *(Oliver Wendell Holmes, Sr.)*

[I would add, "A mind once stretched — by working with and learning from Mitzvah heroes and by committing oneself to Mitzvah projects — …"]

19. No, no, you're not thinking, you're just being logical. *(Niels Bohr)*

[Mitzvah thinking often uses a different part of the brain. We need to develop that part of our cerebral circuitry at least as much as we do our common, logical intelligence.]

20. I want to stay as close to the edge as I can without going over. Out on the edge you see all kinds of things you can't see from the center.

(Kurt Vonnegut)

[In the world of Mitzvahs, though, creative Mitzvah thinking comes from bringing ourselves to view what is fixable and doable in Life above and beyond, sometimes well beyond the norm.]

21.

הקדוש ברוך הוא ליבא בעי

The Holy One wants your heart. *(Sanhedrin 106b)*

22.

א"ד לי....

תְּנָה בְנִי לִבְּךָ לִי

וְעֵינֶיךָ דְּרָכַי תִּרְצֶנָה [תִּצֹּרְנָה].

אמר הקב"ה אי יהבת לי לבך ועיניך אנא ידע דאת לי

Rabbi Levi said:....
It is written,
"Give your heart to me, my child;
Let your eyes watch My ways." *(Proverbs 23:26)*
The Holy One said,
"If you give Me your heart and eyes,
I know you are mine." *(Jerusalem Talmud, Berachot 1:5)*

23. There are people who take the heart out of you,
    and there are people who put it back.
    (Elizabeth David, British Food Writer)

24. I'm not the smartest girl in the world, nor am I the most talented.
    What I have is a heart. *(Nickole Evans)*

25. The heart is revealed in the deed. *(Abraham Joshua Heschel, ז״ל)*

26.
וְכֹל מַה־שֶּׁאֶרְצֶה לְעַצְמִי אֶרְצֶה לוֹ כְּמוֹהוּ
וְכֹל־מַה־שֶּׁלֹּא אֶרְצֶה לְעַצְמִי וְלִידִידִי
לֹא אֶרְצֶה לוֹ בִּשְׁבִילוֹ כְּמוֹהוּ
וְהוּא אָמְרוּ יִתְעַלֶּה
וְאָהַבְתָּ לְרֵעֲךָ כָּמוֹךָ

Whatever I want for myself,
I want the same for that other person.
And whatever I do not want for myself or my friends,
I do not want for that other person.
This is the meaning of the verse,
"And you shall love the other person as yourself." *(Leviticus 19:18)*
(Maimonides, Sefer HaMitzvot,
Positive Mitzvah #206)

27. What we want to change we curse and then pick up a tool.
    Bless whatever you can with eyes and hands and tongue.
    If you can't bless it, get ready to make it new. *(Marge Piercy, poet)*

28.
אַל־תִּמְנַע־טוֹב מִבְּעָלָיו בִּהְיוֹת לְאֵל יָדֶיךָ [יָדְךָ] לַעֲשׂוֹת׃
Do not hold back from doing good for others
When you have the power to do so. *(Proverbs 3:27)*

29.
וַאֲמַר רַבִּי יִצְחָק.....
כָּל הָרוֹדֵף אַחַר צְדָקָה
הַקָּדוֹשׁ בָּרוּךְ הוּא מַמְצִיא לוֹ מָעוֹת וְעוֹשֶׂה בָּהֶן צְדָקָה
רַב נַחְמָן בַּר יִצְחָק אָמַר
הַקָּדוֹשׁ בָּרוּךְ הוּא מַמְצִיא לוֹ בְּנֵי אָדָם הַמְהוּגָּנִים
לַעֲשׂוֹת לָהֶן צְדָקָה

Rabbi Yitzchak said...:
The Holy One will provide sufficient Mitzvah money
for any who runs to do Tzedakah.
Rabbi Nachman bar Yitzchak said:
The Holy One will provide appropriate recipients
through whom to perform the Mitzvah of Tzedakah. *(Bava Batra 9b)*

30. ...some are born great, some achieve greatness, and some have greatness thrust upon them. (*Malvolio, 12th Night, Act II, Scene 5*)

[*A friend of mine used the same rhythms as Shakespeare to express an idea which applies to Tikkun Olam: Some people make things happen, some watch while things happen, and some wonder "What happened?"*]

31.
לְעוֹלָם אֵין אדם מֵעֲנִי מִן הַצְּדָקָה
שֶׁנֶּאֱמַר וְאֵין דָּבָר רַע וְלֹא הֶיזֵק נִגְלָל בִּשְׁבִיל הַצְּדָקָה
וְהָיָה מַעֲשֵׂה הַצְּדָקָה שָׁלוֹם
וַעֲבֹדַת הַצְּדָקָה הַשְׁקֵט וָבֶטַח עַד־עוֹלָם:

No one ever becomes poor from doing Tzedakah.
Nothing bad or harmful comes from doing Tzedakah,
as the verse states,
"The end result of Tzedakah will be peace,
and Tzedakah work will yield
eternal peace-of-mind and security."

(*Maimonides, Hilchot Matnot Ani'im*
[The Laws of Gifts to Poor People 10:2], Isaiah 32:17)
[*The Hebrew term ר ע has a range of meaning which includes everything from not good to toxic to lethal to catastrophic.*]

32.
כִּי־צַדִּיק יְהוָה צְדָקוֹת אָהֵב
God is Righteous; God loves righteous deeds. (*Psalms 11:7*)

33.
פְּעֻלַּת־צַדִּיק לְחַיִּים

(First translation): All of a Good Person's work is for the sake of life.
(Second translation): The work of the Good Person always moves
   in the direction of Life.
(Third translation): The earnings of a Good Person is Life.
(Fourth Translation): The harvest of a Good Person is Life.

(*Proverbs 10:16*)

34.
כֵּן־צְדָקָה לְחַיִּים
Tzedakah gives stability to life. (*Proverbs 11:19*)

35.
וְצַדִּיק יְסוֹד עוֹלָם:

(First translation): The Good Person
   is the very foundation of the world.
(Second translation): The Good Person
   is a foundation that lasts forever. (*Proverbs 10:25*)

36.
עֵת לַחֲבוֹק
אִם רָאִיתָ כַּת שֶׁל צַדִּיקִים עוֹמְדִים עֲמוֹד וְחַבֵּק וְנַשֵּׁק וְגַפְּפָם
"A time to embrace" (*Ecclesiastes 3:5*):
If you see a group of Tzaddikim-Good People standing near you,
stand up and hug them and kiss them and hug them again.

(*Midrash Ecclesiastes Rabba 3:5, 1*)

37.   אַשְׂכִּילָה | בְּדֶרֶךְ תָּמִים

I will study the way of the people whose very essence is innocence.
(Psalm 101:2) (My translation)

I become wise by following the path of the people whose very essence
is innocence. *(Translation by Dr. Abraham J. Gittelson)*

I will study the way of the blameless. *(Jewish Publication Society)*

38.   וְזֹרֵעַ צְדָקָה שֶׂכֶר אֱמֶת׃

A person who sows the seeds of Tzedakah receives a true reward.
                                           (Proverbs 11:18)

39.   איזהו חכם - הרואה את הנולד.

Who is truly wise?
One who can picture not only the immediate, but also the long-term,
effect of what he or she does. *(Tamid 32a)*

40.   הִנֵּה תָּאַבְתִּי לְפִקֻּדֶיךָ בְּצִדְקָתְךָ חַיֵּנִי׃

I love your Mitzvahs.
Give me Life through Your Tzedakah. *(Psalm 119:40)*

41.   בְּפִקֻּדֶיךָ אָשִׂיחָה וְאַבִּיטָה אֹרְחֹתֶיךָ׃

By talking about your Mitzvahs,
I see more clearly the way You would like things to be. *(Psalm 119:15)*

42.   וְאֹרַח צַדִּיקִים כְּאוֹר נֹגַהּ
                                    הוֹלֵךְ וָאוֹר עַד־נְכוֹן הַיּוֹם׃

The path of Good People is like radiant sunlight
Becoming ever brighter until noon. *(Proverbs 4:18)*

43.   וְהַמַּשְׂכִּלִים יַזְהִרוּ כְּזֹהַר הָרָקִיעַ
                     וּמַצְדִּיקֵי הָרַבִּים כַּכּוֹכָבִים לְעוֹלָם וָעֶד׃

People who use their שׂכל/*sechel*, insight-and-talents-for-Mitzvahs
Will be radiant like the bright expanse of the sky,
And those who encourage others to be involved in Tzedakah
Shall be like the eternal stars. *(Daniel 12:3)*

44.   הָעָם הַהֹלְכִים בַּחֹשֶׁךְ רָאוּ אוֹר גָּדוֹל
                     יֹשְׁבֵי בְּאֶרֶץ צַלְמָוֶת אוֹר נָגַהּ עֲלֵיהֶם׃

The people that walked in darkness have seen a brilliant light;
Light has dawned on those who dwelt
in a land of terrifying darkness. *(Isaiah 9:1)*

45.   זָרַח בַּחֹשֶׁךְ אוֹר לַיְשָׁרִים
                                  חַנּוּן וְרַחוּם וְצַדִּיק׃

A light shines in the darkness for upright people;
[The Good Person] is gracious, compassionate, and *Menschlich*.
                                         (Psalm 112:4)

46.   נֵר־לְרַגְלִי דְבָרֶךָ וְאוֹר לִנְתִיבָתִי׃

Your Word is a lamp to my feet,
a light for my path. *(Psalm 119:105)*

47.

אוֹדְךָ עַל כִּי נוֹרָאוֹת נִפְלֵיתִי
נִפְלָאִים מַעֲשֶׂיךָ וְנַפְשִׁי יֹדַעַת מְאֹד׃

I praise You, for I am awesomely, wondrously made;
Your handiwork is breathtaking;
I am profoundly and constantly aware of it. *(Psalm 139:14)*

48.

זכות יש לה קרן ויש לה פירות

Tzedakah has both: principal and interest. *(Tosefta Pe'ah 1:3)*

49.

יָהֵב חָכְמְתָא לְחַכִּימִין

God gives wisdom to wise people. *(Daniel 2:21)*

50. There must be more to life than having everything. *(Maurice Sendak)*

51. When I ask myself how it happened that I in particular discovered the Relativity Theory, it seemed to lie in the following circumstance. The normal adult never bothers his head about space-time problems. Everything there is to be thought about, in his opinion, has already been done in early childhood. I, on the contrary, developed so slowly that I only began to wonder about space and time when I was already grown up. In consequence, I probed deeper into the prob-lem than an ordinary child would have done. *(Albert Einstein)*

52. Mitzvahs are like potato chips. Just as you can't eat only one potato chip, so, too, you can't just do one Mitzvah — your appetite and urge to do more of them just keeps growing. *(Unknown Source)*

53. Boundless dreams,
Heroic goals.
High Standards, and
Rich blessings.

(The Reverend Linda Tarry-Chard,
Co-Founder of The Project People Foundation)

54.

רב אמ' לא נתנו מצוות אלא לצרוף בהן את הבריריות

Rav said: The Mitzvot were given in order to refine human beings.
(Leviticus Rabba 13:3 [Margoliot Edition])

55.

רב אמר לא נתנו המצות לישראל אלא לצרף בהן את הבריות

Rav said:
The Mitzvot were given in order to tie God's creatures together.
(Leviticus Rabba 13:3)

56. Treat a man as he is, and he will remain as he is.
Treat a man as he could be, and he will become what he should be.
(Ralph Waldo Emerson)

57. The opposite of love is not hate, it's indifference.
The opposite of faith is not heresy, it's indifference.
And, the opposite of life is not death, it's indifference.
Because of indifference one dies before one actually dies.

(Elie Wiesel)

58.

אָמַר רַבָּה
כִּי מִיפַּטְרִי רַבָּנָן מֵהֲדָדֵי בְּפוּמְבְּדִיתָא אָמְרִי הָכִי
מַחֵיה חַיִּים
יִתֵּן לָךְ חַיִּים אֲרוּכִים וְטוֹבִים וּמְתוּקָנִין

Rabbah said,
When the Torah students in Pumpeditha would part from each other,
they would say,
"May God, Who gives Life to the living,
give you a long and good and stable life." *(Yoma 71a)*

59.

מָה אֲנִי בּוֹרֵא עוֹלָמוֹת וּמְחַיֶּה מֵתִים
אַף אַתֶּם כֵּן

[God says:] Just as I create worlds and bring the dead back to life,
you, human beings, are also capable of doing the same.

(Midrash Psalms 116:8)

60.

וְאָהַבְתָּ לְרֵעֲךָ כָּמוֹךָ
רַבִּי עֲקִיבָא אוֹמֵר זֶה כְּלָל גָּדוֹל בַּתּוֹרָה.
בֶּן עַזַּאי אוֹמֵר
זֶה סֵפֶר תּוֹלְדֹת אָדָם
זֶה כְּלָל גָּדוֹל מִזֶּה

"Love your neighbor as yourself," *(Leviticus 19:18)* —
Rabbi Akiva says,
"This is the all-encompassing Torah-principle."
Ben Azzai says,
"'This is the story of humanity:
[When God created the first human being,
God created that person in the likeness of God]' *(Genesis 5:1)*
is an even greater principle." *(Sifra, Kedoshim, on Leviticus 19:18)*

61. We make a living by what we get,
but we make a life by what we give. *(Winston Churchill)*

62. There are only two ways to live your life.
One is as though nothing is a miracle.
The other is as though everything is a miracle. *(Albert Einstein)*

63. Mature your minds with great thoughts;
to believe in the heroic makes heroes. *(Benjamin Disraeli)*

64. What lies behind us and what lies before us are tiny matters
compared to what lies within us. *(Ralph Waldo Emerson)*

65.

רֹדֵף צְדָקָה וָחָסֶד יִמְצָא חַיִּים צְדָקָה וְכָבוֹד:

A person who runs to do Tzedakah
and to perform just, good, and kind deeds
attains Life, success, and honor. *(Proverbs 21:21)*

66.

טוֹב לִיתֵּן צְדָקָה קוֹדֶם תְּפִלָּה

It is good to give Tzedakah before praying.
(Shulchan Aruch, Orach Chaim 92:10)

116

67.

אמר רבי חייא בר אבא
לעולם יתפלל אדם בבית שיש בו חלונות

Rabbi Chiyya bar Abba said:
You should always pray in a place where there are windows.

(Berachot 34b)

68.

כִּי יְדַעְתִּיו לְמַעַן אֲשֶׁר יְצַוֶּה אֶת־בָּנָיו וְאֶת־בֵּיתוֹ אַחֲרָיו
וְשָׁמְרוּ דֶּרֶךְ יְהֹוָה לַעֲשׂוֹת צְדָקָה וּמִשְׁפָּט

For I have selected him [Abraham]
so that he may instruct his children and his posterity after him
to keep God's ways:
to do what is just and right. [Tzedakah U'Mishpat] *(Genesis 18:19)*

69. Three things in human life are important:
The first is to be kind.
The second is to be kind.
And the third is to be kind. *(Henry James)*

70. It takes courage for a man to listen to his own goodness and act on it.
(Norman Cousins)

71. Living is not a private affair of the individual.
Living is what man does with God's time,
what man does with God's world.

(Rabbi Abraham Joshua Heschel, ז״ל)

72. The meaning of man's life lies in his perfecting the universe. He has to distinguish…and redeem the sparks of holiness scattered throughout the darkness of the world.

(Rabbi Abraham Joshua Heschel, ז״ל)

73. I would say to young people a number of things….I would say let them remember that there is meaning beyond absurdity. Let them be sure that every little deed counts, that every word has power, and that we can, everyone, do our share to redeem the world in spite of all absurdities and all the frustrations and all disappointments.

(Rabbi Abraham Joshua Heschel, ז״ל)

74.

דרש ר' שמלאי
תורה תחלתה גמילות חסדים וסופה גמילות חסדים

Rabbi Simla'i explained in a sermon:
The Torah begins and ends with acts of caring, loving kindness.

(Sotah 14a)

75. This is happiness: to be dissolved into something completely great.
(Willa Cather)

76. How wonderful it is that no one need wait a single moment to start to improve the world. *(Anne Frank)*

77. When you take a stand, it shapes who you are. It sets your priori-ties. It wakes you up in the morning, and it dresses you. It puts you to bed at night. There's deep spirituality in that way of being.
(Lynne Twist, Founding Executive Director of The Hunger Project)

78. לָכֵן כֹּה־אָמַר יְהֹוָה...וְאִם־תּוֹצִיא יָקָר מִזּוֹלֵל כְּפִי תִהְיֶה
Assuredly, thus says God:...
If you produce what is noble out of what is worthless,
You shall be My spokesperson. *(Jeremiah 15:19)*

79. לֹא ישתמש אדם בפניו ידיו ורגליו אלא לכבוד קונהו
One should use one's face, hands, and feet
only to honor one's Creator. *(Tosefta Brachot 4:1)*

80. Maybe I'm a fool, but I believe that dignity wins out.
When it doesn't, then we as a people become extinct.
(Roy Stryker, The Depression Photography Project)

81. ...כל אחד ואחד חייב לומר, בשבילי נברא העולם
...every single person is required to say,
"The whole world was created for my sake."
(Mishnah Sanhedrin, end of chapter 4)

82. A billion here, a billion there, pretty soon it adds up to real money.
(Senator Everett Dirksen)

[Senator Dirksen was referring to the enormous sums allocated by Congress for government programs. With Tikkun Olam, people know that emptying even a few pennies from a Tzedakah box/pushka and donating it wisely can have earthshaking and lifesaving consequences.]

83. It's not what you are, but what you don't become that hurts.
(Oscar Levant)

84. When the great, sweet Rabbi Zusia of Hanipol was on his death-bed, his students gathered all around him. The Teacher said to them:
When I get to the Next World, I am not afraid if God will ask me, "Zusia, why weren't you Moses, to lead the people out of this land where Jews are so oppressed and beaten by the people?" I can answer, "I did not have the leadership abilities of a Moses."
And if God asks, "Zusia, why weren't you Isaiah, reprimanding the people for their sins and urging them to change their ways, to repent?" I could answer, "I did not have the eloquence of Isaiah, the Great Master of power-ful and dazzling speech."
And if God should ask, "Zusia, why weren't you Maimonides, to explain the deeper meaning of Judaism to the philosophers of the world, so they would un-derstand the Jews better and perhaps treat them better?" I can answer, "I did not have the vast intellectual skills of Maimonides."
No, my students, I am not afraid of those questions. What I fear is this: What if God asks me, "Zusia, why weren't you Zusia?"
Then what will I say? *(Chassidic Tale)*

85. Maimonides' 8 Levels of Tzedakah

שמנה מעלות יש בצדקה זו למעלה מזו,
מעלה גדולה שאין למעלה ממנה זה המחזיק ביד ישראל שמך
ונותן לו מתנה או הלואה או עושה עמו שותפות או ממציא לו מלאכה
כדי לחזק את ידו עד שלא יצטרך לבריות לשאול,
ועל זה נאמר והחזקת בו גר ותושב וחי עמך
כלומר החזק בו עד שלא יפול ויצטרך.
ח פחות מזה הנותן צדקה לעניים
ולא ידע למי נתן ולא ידע העני ממי לקח,
שהרי זו מצוה לשמה, כגון לשכת חשאים שהיתה במקדש,
שהיו הצדיקים נותנין בה בחשאי
והעניים בני טובים מתפרנסין ממנה בחשאי,
וקרוב לזה הנותן לתוך קופה של צדקה,
ולא יתן אדם לתוך קופה של צדקה
אלא אם כן יודע שהממונה נאמן וחכם
ויודע להנהיג כשורה כר' חנניה בן תרדיון.
ט פחות מזה שידע הנותן למי יתן ולא ידע העני ממי לקח,
כגון גדולי החכמים שהיו הולכין בסתר
ומשליכין המעות בפתחי העניים.
וכזה ראוי לעשות ומעלה טובה היא
אם אין הממונין בצדקה נוהגין כשורה.
י פחות מזה שידע העני ממי נטל ולא ידע הנותן,
כגון גדולי החכמים שהיו צוררים המעות בסדיניהן ומפשילין לאחוריהן
ובאין העניים ונוטלין כדי שלא יהיה להן בושה.
יא פחות מזה שיתן לו בידו קודם שישאל.
יב פחות מזה שיתן לו אחר שישאל.
יג פחות מזה שיתן לו פחות מן הראוי בסבר פנים יפות.
יד פחות מזה שיתן לו בעצב.

There are eight levels of giving Tzedakah:

1. The highest level is to strengthen the hand of a Jew who is poor, giving that person a gift, or a loan, or becoming a partner, or finding a job for that person, to strengthen the person's hand, so that the person can become self-supporting...

2. A lower level is a person who gives Tzedakah to the poor and is unaware of the recipient, who in turn is unaware of the giver. This is indeed a religious act achieved for its own sake.
   Of a similar character is one who contributes to a Tzedakah fund. One should not contribute to a Tzedakah fund unless he or she knows that the person in charge of the collections is trustworthy and intelligent and knows how to manage the money properly...

3. The third, lesser, level is when the giver knows the recipient, but the recipient does not know the giver. The great sages used to go secretly and cast the money into the doorway of poor people. Something like this should be done, it being a noble virtue, if the Tzedakah administrators are behaving properly.

4. The fourth, still lower level is when the recipient knows the giver, but the giver does not know the recipient. The great sages used to tie money in sheets which they threw behind their backs, and poor people would come and get it without being embarrassed.

5. The fifth level is when the giver puts the Tzedakah money into the hands of poor people without being asked.

6. The sixth level is when he or she puts the money into the hands of a poor person after being solicited.

7. The seventh level is when he or she gives the poor person less than he or she should, but does so cheerfully.

8. The eighth level is when he or she gives the poor person grudgingly/with a feeling of pain/unhappily.

(Mishna Torah, Laws of Gifts to Poor People, 10:7-14)

Readings You May Find Useful At The Great Event

**(Poems and Translations by the Author.
Poems with Italics may be read responsively.)**

A Blessing

Berachot 17a
Eruvin 54a

May your eyes sparkle with the light of Torah,
and may your ears hear the music of its words.
May the space between each letter of the scrolls
bring warmth and happiness to your soul.
May the syllables draw holiness from your heart,
and may this holiness be gentle and soothing
to you and all God's creatures.
May your study be passionate,
and meanings bear more meanings
until Life itself arrays itself before you
as a dazzling wedding feast.
And may your conversation,
even of the commonplace,
be a blessing to all who listen to your words
and see the Torah glowing on your face.

A Rebbi's Proverb

(From the Yiddish)

If you always assume
        the person sitting next to you
                is the Messiah
        waiting for some simple human kindness —

You will soon come to weigh your words
        and watch your hands.

And if the person chooses
        not to be revealed
                in your time —

It will not matter.

The Good People

The Good People everywhere
will teach anyone who wants to know
how to fix all things breaking and broken in this world —
including hearts and dreams —
and along the way we will learn such things as
why we are here
and what we are supposed to be doing
with our hands and minds and souls and our time.
That way, we can hope to find out why
we were given a human heart,
and that way, we can hope to know
the hearts of other human beings
and the heart of the world.

The Restaurant of Broken Dreams

It came to seem that
wherever he went
everything was broken.
Even when he chanced upon a place,
it was a matter of most everything in pieces,
the largest thing whole being no bigger than a vase
or a small handbag without a tear or scratch.
As he spoke to people,
he heard there, too, lines like,
"This is the street of broken dreams."
"This is the restaurant of broken dreams."
"There is the car of broken dreams."
And so he set himself to find the best carpenters,
experts in porcelain and ceramics, insulation and leather,
people who knew how to mend garden hoses
as well as surgeons fixed arteries, plumbers.
He learned each trade in turn
and drew each of his teachers into
what came to be known as
The Great Fixing in the Land.
When he died,
bits and splinters had become endangered species,
and little children with glue and tape and nails in their hands
surrounded his bed and promised to carry on his work,
and their parents awoke each morning,
their dreams still whole.

Two Prayers From the Talmud

ר' יוחנן הוה מצלי
יהי רצון מלפניך ה' אלהי ואלהי אבותי
שתשכן בפוריינו אהבה ואחוה שלום וריעות
ותצליח סופינו אחרית ותקוה ותרבה גבולנו בתלמידים
ונשיש בחלקינו בג"ע ותקנינו לב טוב וחבר טוב
ונשכים ונמצא ייחול לבבינו
ותבא לפניך קורת נפשינו לטובה

May it be Your will, O my God
    and God of my ancestors,
to grace our lives with love
    and a feeling for the intimacy of all humanity
and peace and friendship,
    and may all our days flourish because we are hopeful,
and may the borders of our lives overflow with students,
    and may we enjoy our reward in Paradise.
Arrange things so that we will have good hearts
    and good friends,
and allow us to awaken with our appropriate yearnings fulfilled,
    and may You consider our wishes to be decent-and-good.

        (Rabbi Yochanan's prayer,
        Jerusalem Talmud, Berachot 4:2)

רב אלכסנדרי בתר צלותיה אמר הכי
יהי רצון מלפניך ה' אלהינו
שתעמידנו בקרן אורה ואל תעמידנו בקרן חשכה.
ואל ידוה לבנו ואל יחשכו עינינו.

May it be Your will, O our God,
that we be allowed to stand in places of astonishing light
and not in dark places,
and may our hearts know no pain,
and may our vision not be so clouded
[that we would not see all the blessings of Life
that You have given us.]

        (Rabbi Alexandrai's prayer,
        Babylonian Talmud, Berachot 17a)

Mitzvah Therapy

Then let us, troubled, do this:
raise finches and parakeets for all Old Ones living all alone;
tend plants and flowers,
violets and geraniums, impatiens, pansies, and irises,
and roses of every color
to grow to give to The Lonely People of this world
that they may have the will to awaken tomorrow and live;
teach dogs to pull wheelchairs
when there is no power in the human's legs
to stand or to walk,
train them to run to their owners
when there is someone knocking at the door
but there is no hearing to hear; groom horses,
Quarter Horses and Shetlands and Appaloosas,
that will, in their mass and rhythms, and displaying their style,
trot and canter and gallop
and bring dead limbs back to their rightful lives;
let us clean their stables and pitch their hay
and haul their water to the troughs
so they may be mighty Mitzvah steeds
for, though we drop from exhaustion,
we will have done our part;
tune cars at cost or for free
for all those who live so close to the edge of poverty they despair
when all they need
is nothing more than a wreck with four wheels
to take them to work
— *for anyone who has only one last chance left;*
collect millions of pennies,
count them and roll them and give them away;
be World Class Huggers
overcoming our fear of touch;
paint the planes that fly hearts and lungs and kidneys
up and down the coast and cross-country
and everywhere in between
wherever the ones who live in desperation are waiting,
in the blazing colors of hope;
clown in the hospitals,
do some things all good.

Courage

You dare to call us partners;
>We will live, one day at a time,
>>performing signs and wonders for the benefit of others.
>>>*This we promise You.*

You dare to call us little lower than the angels;
>We will use our face and hands to be Your messengers.
>>*To this we commit ourselves this day.*

You dare to tell us we are fashioned in Your image;
>We will be this Image, live our lives
>by the most Divine in us,
>and in this Image listen to Your words and do Your will.
>>*So we solemnly declare this day.*

Your Mitzvah opportunities await.
>*Give us strength: we vow to do Your will*
>*as, by Your light and guidance,*
>*our hearts and souls so move us.*

What You Find

This is what you find
if you live long enough
and if you know where to look
and it is not far,
and the search is not wearing
when you know where to look:
the best.
By which I mean:
people.
By which I mean:
in the people,
some more, some less,
a spark.
By which I mean:
tinder and kindling and glowing coals from Above
scattered,
invisibly small,
and, once in the soul, they burn,
and the face glows.
You do not have to travel as far as I have
to see the faces.
Warm your soul by the fire.

Psalm 24, To Fashion Holiness

O God —
Show us how to fashion
holiness from waste,
discovering sparks in the broken shells
of people beaten down by circumstance
and mired in the boredom of hollowness.

Teach us to take
the neutral substance of reality
and create the sublime,
forming shapes of blessings
with a sacred touch.

Instruct us in sympathy,
so we may learn to tear away at hopelessness
and the groan and oy of despair
by stories, jokes, and astonishing embraces.

Remove shallowness from our lives
and destroy senselessness,
that we may discover Your plan
and fulfill Your purposes.

Give us insight and vision,
and we will perform signs and wonders
in the sight of all humanity
as You Yourself once did
in the Land of Egypt and at Sinai.

Show us Life in all its glory,
and we will glorify Your name,
here and now, everywhere and forever.

A Prayer of Responsibility for Children

We pray for children who put chocolate fingers everywhere, who like to be tickled, who stomp in puddles and ruin their new pants, who sneak popsicles before supper, who erase holes in math workbooks, who can never find their shoes...

And we pray for those who stare at photographers from behind barbed wire, who can't bound down the street in a new pair of sneakers, who never "counted potatoes, who are born in places in which we wouldn't be caught dead, who never go to the circus, who live in an X-rated world.

We pray for children who bring us sticky kisses and fistfuls of dandelions, who sleep with the dog and bury goldfish, who hug us in a hurry and forget their lunch money, who cover themselves with Band-aids and sing off key, who squeeze toothpaste all over the sink, who slurp their soup.

And we pray for those who never get dessert, who have no safe blanket to drag behind them, who watch their parents watch them die, who can't find any bread to steal, who don't have any rooms to clean up, whose pictures aren't on any-body's dresser, whose monsters are real...

We pray for children who spend all their allowance before Tuesday, who throw tantrums in the grocery store and pick their food, who like ghost stories, who shove dirty clothes under the bed and never rinse out the tub, who love visits from the tooth fairy, who don't like to be kissed in front of the school bus, who squirm in church or temple and scream in the phone...

And we pray for those whose nightmares come in the day-time, who will eat anything, who have never seen a dentist, who aren't spoiled by anybody, who go to bed hungry and cry themselves to sleep, who live and move and have no being.

We pray for children who want to be carried and for those who must, for those we never give up on and for those who will grab the hand of anyone kind enough to offer it.

Hear our cries, Adonai, and listen to our prayers. Amen.

(Reprinted with permission by the author, Ina J. Hughs)

How To Treat Holiness

Where holiness hides in shadow, bring the light.
With holiness,
be strong and comforting.
Set it at ease, holiness.
Embrace it if it is lonely,
Hug it strong and soft
at once.
Let it walk with you in your own footsteps
when you walk by the way,
and shimmer in your face
when you lie down and when you rise up.
In your being, be for the sake of Heaven.

Give of your money, the tool of justice and compassion,
and stretch your arms full stretch to those who suffer
as the Almighty God did for us
when all Pharaohs were brought low in our own sight.
The ways of Tzedakah are pleasantness,
and all the paths of Mitzvahs are peace.
Give of yourselves and thereby be yourselves.
Be strong.
Love God.
Love the People Israel,
and be you holy unto them.
God may be with you.

God is with you.

1.   חד איתתא הוות רחמא מצוותא סגיא

[The printed text reads: רחמנא. The late Talmudic genius, Professor Saul Lieberman, ז"ל, corrected the text to read רח מא, as written above.]

2.   תניא היה רבי מאיר אומר חייב אדם לברך מאה ברכות בכל יום

It was taught:

Rabbi Meir says, "Everyone is required to make 100 blessings every day."

3.   רב אמ' לא נתנו מצוות אלא לצרוף בהן את הבריריות

Rav said: Mitzvahs were given in order to refine human beings.

4.   היה הוא צריך ללמוד ויש לו בן ללמוד
ואין ידו משגת להספיק לשניהם אם שניהם שוים הוא קודם לבנו

If a parent wished to study Torah, and there is a child who must also study,
and the parent doesn't have enough money for both,
the parent takes precedence.

5.   דרש רבי שמלאי...
ואינו יוצא משם עד שמשביעין אותו....
ומה היא השבועה שמשביעין אותו
תהי צדיק ואל תהי רשע

Rabbi Simla'i gave the following sermon…:

It does not leave the womb until it is made to swear an oath.

And what is that oath?

"Be a good person [Mensch], and do not be a bad person."

6.   אל"ף בי"ת אלף בינה גימ"ל דל"ת גמול דלים

7.   פתחו לי שערי צדק לעולם הבא אמרו לו לאדם מה היה מלאכתך
והוא אומר מאכיל רעבים הייתי
והם יאמרו לו זה השער לה' מאכיל רעבים הכנס בו
משקה צמאים הייתי והם אומרים לו זה השער לה' משקה צמאים הכנס בו
מלביש ערומים הייתי והם אומרים לו זה השער לה' מלביש ערומים הכנס בו
וכן מגדל יתומים וכן עושי צדקה וכן גומלי חסדים

"Open the Gates of Righteousness [Justice, Victory] for me,..."

(Psalm 118:19)

[At the Time of Judgment] in the Future World,

everyone will be asked, "What was your occupation?"

If the person answers, "I used to feed hungry people," they will say to that person,

"This is God's gate, you, who fed hungry people, may enter."...

"I used to give water to thirsty people," they will say to that person,

"This is God's gate, you, who gave water to those who were thirsty may enter."...

"I used to give clothing to those who needed clothing," they will say to that person,

"This is God's gate, you, who gave clothing to those who needed clothing,
     may enter."...

and, similarly, those who raised orphans,

and who performed the Mitzvah of Tzedakah,

and who performed acts of caring, loving kindness.

(Taught to me by Rabbi Matthew Simon.)

8.

שיעור נתינתה אם ידו משגת יתן כפי צורך העניים
ואם אין ידו משגת כל כך יתן עד חומש נכסיו מצוה מן המובחר
ואחד מעשרה מדה בינונית פחות מכאן עין רעה...
הגה ואל יבזבז אדם יותר מחומש שלא יצטרך לבריות

The amount one should give to Tzedakah:
If one can afford it, enough to answer all the needs of the poor people.
But if one cannot afford that much, then
one should give up to a fifth of one's possessions —
which is doing the Mitzvah in an exceptional fashion —
one tenth is an average percentage,
and less is considered miserly (poor eyesight)....
[Gloss by Rabbi Moshe Isserles:]
And one should not give away more than 20%,
lest he or she ultimately become dependent on others.

9. Rabbi Casper is willing to help you decide what will work best for your own flower or plant Mitzvah project. Contact him at SurfFlorist@juno.com. [www.miamibeachflowers.com]

10. In an article called "Risk-Free Food Donations" in Meetings and Conventions Magazine (Reed Publishing, Secaucus, NJ), Mr. Jonathan Howe of the Chicago law firm Howe & Hutton Ltd., composed a written agreement between the donor organization and the recipient charity. It offers a greater element of protection (and peace of mind) to the donor. Mr. Howe would be happy to answer any questions about this Indemnification Agreement. 312-263-3002, fax: 312-372-6685. This is the text of his proposed agreement, reproduced by permission of Mr. Howe:

INDEMNIFICATION AGREEMENT

AGREEMENT
Agreement, entered into this ___ day of _____, 200_, by and between [insert name and address of event sponsor, which is the ORGANIZATION] and [insert name and address of charity or food recipient, which is the CHARITY].
RECITALS
        ORGANIZATION desires to donate food and non-alcoholic beverages not uti-lized at its meetings and other gatherings to CHARITY.
        CHARITY desires to receive donations of food and non-alcoholic beverages not utilized by ORGANIZATION for distribution to CHARITY.
IT IS AGREED:
In consideration of the donation of food and non-alcoholic beverages made to it by ORGANIZATION, CHARITY, shall, to the extent not otherwise provided by the law of the States, indemnify, defend, and hold harmless ORGANIZATION, its officers, directors, employees, agents, and members, and each of them, from and against any and all loss, damage, claim, liability, injury, illness or death, including costs of defense, caused by or arising from ORGANIZATION's donation of food and non-alcoholic beverages to CHARITY.

[Insert name of ORGANIZATION]
By _____
Its _____

[Insert name of CHARITY]
By _____
Its _____

11.   כל דבר שמביאין לפני האדם שיש לו ריח והאדם תאב לו
צריך ליתן ממנו לשמש מיד
ומדת חסידות הוא ליתן לו מיד מכל מין ומין

Whatever food that is served that has an aroma and that awakens the appetite
should be given to the waitstaff immediately. And it is a particularly Menschlich
human quality to immediately give the waitstaff some of every kind of food being
served.

12.   אלא חוט של תכלת מאי היא?
דתניא, היה ר"מ אומר מה נשתנה תכלת מכל מיני צבעונין?
מפני שהתכלת דומה לים, וים דומה לרקיע,
ורקיע דומה לכסא הכבוד, שנאמר (שמות כד)
ויראו את אלהי ישראל ותחת רגליו
כמעשה לבנת הספיר וכעצם השמים לטהר,

13.   קונם כהנים ולוים נהנים לי, יטלו על כרחו.

I vow that the Kohanim and Levi'im should have no benefit
    from anything that is mine,
They [the Kohanim and Levi'im] take [their Terumah and Ma'aser anyway...
(even against the farmer's will, because these portions of the crop do not belong to
— never belonged to — the farmer. They always belonged to the Kohanim and
Levi'im.)

14. Healthy Reasons to Have a Pet

Abstracts or copies of most of the articles referenced below are available in the
Health Benefits of Animals section of the website www.deltasociety.org.

- Animal-assisted therapy can effectively reduce the loneliness of residents in
  long-term care facilities. (Banks, 2002).
- People with borderline hypertension had lower blood pressure on days they
  took their dogs to work. (Allen, K. 2001).
- Seniors who own dogs go to the doctor less than those who do not. In a
  study of 100 Medicare patients, even the most highly stressed dog owners in
  the study has 21 percent fewer physician's contacts than non-dog owners.
  (Siegel, 1990).
- Activities of daily living (ADL) level of seniors who did not currently own
  pets deteriorated more on average than that of respondents who currently
  owned pets. (Raina, 1999).
- Seniors who own pets coped better with stress life events without entering
  the healthcare system. (Raina, 1998).
- Pet owners have lower blood pressure. (Friedmann, 1983, Anderson 1992).
- Pet owners have lower triglyceride and cholesterol levels than non-owners
  (Anderson, 1992).
- ACE inhibitors lower resting blood pressure but they do not diminish reactivity to mental stress. Pet ownership can lessen cardiovascular reactivity to
  psychological stress among hypertensive patients treated with a daily dose
  of Lisinopril. (Allen, 1999).
- Companionship of pets (particularly dogs) helps children in families adjust
  better to the serious illness and death of a parent (Raveis, 1993).
- Pet owners feel less afraid of being a victim of crime when walking with a

dog or sharing a residence with a dog. (Serpel, 1990).

- Pet owners have fewer minor health problems (Friedmann, 1990, Serpel, 1990).
- Pet owners have better psychological well-being (Serpel, 1990).
- Contact with pets develops nurturing behavior in children who may grow to be more nurturing adults (Melson, 1990).
- Pet owners have higher on-year survival rates following coronary heart disease (Friedman, 1980, 1995).
- Medication costs dropped from an average of $3.80 per patient per day to just $1.18 per patient per day in new nursing home facilities in New York, Missouri and Texas that have animals and plants as an integral part of the environment. (Montague, 1995).
- Pets in nursing homes increase social and verbal interactions adjunct to other therapy. (Fick, 1992).
- Pet owners have better physical health due to exercise with their pets. (Serpel, 1990).
- Having a pet may decrease heart attack mortality by 3%. This translates into 30,000 lives saved annually (Friedman, 1980).
- Dogs are preventive and therapeutic measures against everyday stress (Allen, 1991).
- Pets decrease feeling of loneliness and isolation (Kidd, 1994).
- Children exposed to humane education programs display enhanced empathy for humans compared with children not exposed to such programs. (Ascione, 1992).
- Positive self-esteem of children is enhanced by owning a pet. (Bergensen, 1989).
- Children's cognitive development can be enhanced by owning a pet. (Poresky, 1988).
- 70% of families surveyed reported an increase in family happiness and fun subsequent to pet acquisition. (Cain, 1985).
- The presence of a dog during a child's physical examination decreases their stress. (Nadgengast, 1997, Baun, 1998).
- Children owning pets are more involved in activities such as sports, hobbies, clubs or chores. (Melson, 1990).
- Children exposed to pets during the first year of life have a lower frequency of allergic rhinitis and asthma. (Hesselmar, 1999).
- Children with autism who have contact with pets have more prosocial behaviors and less autistic behaviors such as self-absorption. (Redefer, 1989).
- Children who own pets score significantly higher on empathy and prosocial orientation scales than non-owners. (Vidovic, 1999).
- Pets fulfill many of the same support functions as humans for adults and children. (Melson, 1998).
- People who have AIDS that have pets have less depression and reduced stress. Pets are a major source of support and increase perception the ability to cope. (Siegel, 1999, Carmack, 1991).

picture by Guy Raivitz

Danny Siegel

Danny Siegel is a well-known author, lecturer, and poet who has spoken in more than 300 North American Jewish communities, to synagogues, JCC's, Federations, and other communal organizations on Tzedakah and Jewish values, besides reading from his own poetry. He is the author of numerous books on such topics as Mitzvah heroes and practical and personalized Tzedakah, as well as several books of poetry.

Siegel is sometimes referred to as "The World's Greatest Expert on Microphilanthropy," "The Feeling Person's Thinker," and "The Pied Piper of Tzedakah."

His most recent books in prose include *1 + 1 = 3 and 37 Other Mitzvah Principles For a Meaningful Life, Heroes and Miracle Workers,* and *Good People,* collections of essays about everyday people who are Mitzvah heroes and great Menschen, *Mitzvah Magic — What Kids Can Do To Change the World* and *Tell Me a Mitzvah,* Tzedakah stories for children ages 7-12.

Ziv Tzedakah Fund, the non-profit Mitzvah organization he founded in 1981, has distributed more than $7,000,000 to worthy individuals and projects.

Siegel has a B.S. in Comparative Literature from Columbia University's School of General Studies, and a Bachelor's and Master's of Hebrew Literature from the Jewish Theological Seminary of America.

He is one of three recipients of the prestigious 1993 Covenant Award for Exceptional Jewish Educators.

Notes and Reminders

Notes and Reminders

Notes and Reminders

Notes and Reminders